cute & easy
crocheted cozies

cute & easy
crocheted cozies

35 simply stylish projects to make and give

Nicki Trench

CICO BOOKS

LONDON NEW YORK

Published in 2016 by CICO Books
An imprint of Ryland Peters & Small Ltd
341 E 116th St, New York, NY 10029

www.rylandpeters.com

10 9 8 7 6 5 4 3 2 1

A CIP catalog record for this book is available from the
Library of Congress.

ISBN: 978 1 78249 332 7

Printed in China

Editor: Marie Clayton
Designer: Barbara Zuniga
Photographer: Gavin Kingcome
Stylist: Sophie Martell and Nel Haynes
Illustrator: Stephen Dew

In-house editor: Anna Galkina
Art Director: Sally Powell
Production controller: Sarah Kulasek-Boyd
Publishing Manager: Penny Craig
Publisher: Cindy Richards

contents

introduction

Once upon a time, cozies were confined to teapots and hot water bottles, but with all the technological devices now in our households we can take much pleasure making cozies for just about anything that needs protection. In this collection there are cozies for cellphones (pages 30 and 46), laptops (pages 32 and 40), tablets (pages 26 and 44), and eBook readers (page 34). There is a very cute Baby Cozy with a hood and ears (page 78), cafetière cozies (pages 66 and 88), a Glasses Cozy (page 106), and even a Cold Bottle Cozy (page 68) that you can take to the gym—you'll never have to worry about getting your bottle mixed up with someone else's ever again!

Devices and containers come in all different shapes and sizes, so all the patterns in this book are suggested measurements. Where possible I have given stitch multiples in the patterns, so you can adjust the size of your cozy to fit your own item. I have chosen the yarns for their yummy colors and textures—and for how easy they are to crochet with. Most cozies work well in a light worsted (DK) yarn, or something even thicker for more protection, but for cozies that are purely decorative—such as the Vase Cozies on page 64—I have a used a fine laceweight yarn with beautiful colors to show the light coming through the glass jars.

Most cozies are made to protect, so I have lined many of the items with a cotton fabric and used some thicker, textured stitches: a puff stitch for the Striped Laptop Cozy (page 40) and a bobble stitch for the Bobble Cafetière Cozy (page 88). If you would like the cozy even thicker you could also add some batting between the lining and the crochet, but take care not to make the cozy too bulky. I pop my laptop into a cozy and then into my purse and—although I want it to be protected—I don't want the cozy to take up all the space (I need to keep a hook and yarn in there too!).

In this book we also have a techniques section on pages 8-23, and there are also many tips and notes to help you along when reading the patterns. One of the instructions that is used often in most of the patterns, particularly when a color change is necessary, is: "Cut yarn, do not fasten off." When doing this keep the hook in the loop, cut the yarn approximately 4in. (10cm) from the loop on the hook, and then join the next color as instructed.

Once you start thinking of all the items you can cover with a crochet cozy you will get obsessed and want to crochet a cover for just about everything! I hope you have as much enjoyment making the projects in this book as I did designing them for you. Enjoy.

techniques

basic stitches

Crochet has only a few basic stitches and once you've mastered these all extended stitches follow the same principles. Practice the basic stitches before attempting your first pattern. Crochet is easy to undo because you only have one loop on the hook so you can't really go wrong. When practicing keep the loops loose—you can work on creating an even gauge across the fabric later.

Holding your hook and yarn

Holding the yarn and hook correctly is a very important part of crochet and once you have practiced this it will help you to create your stitches at an even gauge.

Holding your hook

There are two basic ways of holding the hook. I always teach the pen position as I find this more comfortable. It gives you a more relaxed arm and shoulder.

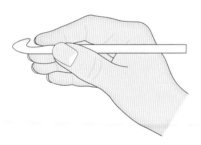 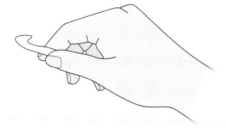 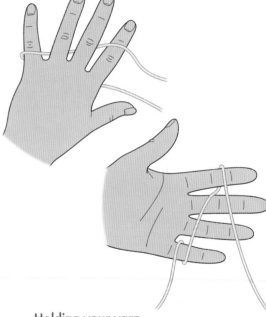

Pen position Pick up your hook as though you are picking up a pen or pencil. Keeping the hook held loosely between your fingers and thumb, turn the hook so that the tip is facing up and the hook is balanced in your hand and resting in the space between your index finger and your thumb.

Knife position But if I'm using a very large hook and chunky yarn, then I may sometimes change and use the knife position. I crochet a lot and I've learned that it's important to take care not to damage your arm or shoulder by being too tense. Make sure you're always relaxed when crocheting and take breaks.

Holding your yarn
Pick up the yarn with your little finger on the opposite hand to the hook, with palm facing toward you, the short end in front of the finger and the yarn in the crease between little finger and ring finger. Turn your hand to face downward (see above top), placing the long yarn strand on top of your index finger, under the other two fingers and wrapped right around the little finger. Then turn your hand to face you (above bottom), ready to hold the work in your middle finger and thumb.

Holding hook and yarn while crocheting

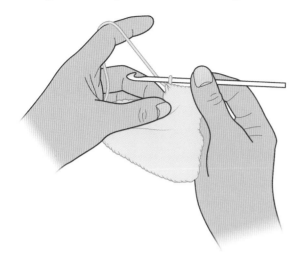

Keep your index finger, with the yarn draped over it, at a slight curve, and hold your work (or the slip knot) using the same hand, between your middle finger and your thumb and just below the crochet hook and loop/s on the hook. As you draw the loop through the hook release the yarn on the index finger to allow the loop to stay loose on the hook. If you tense your index finger, the yarn will become too tight and will pull the loop on the hook too tight for you to draw the yarn through.

Holding hook and yarn for left-handers

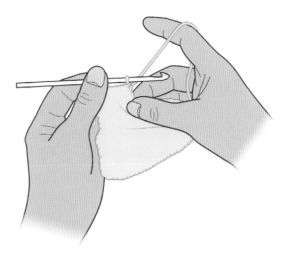

Some left-handers learn to crochet like right-handers, but others learn with everything reversed—with the hook in the left hand and the yarn in the right hand.

Slip knot

A slip knot is the loop that you put onto the hook to start any stitch in crochet.

1 Make a circle of yarn as shown.

2 In one hand hold the circle at the top where the yarn crosses, and let the tail drop down at the back so that it falls across the center of the loop. With your free hand, or the tip of a crochet hook, pull a loop through the circle.

3 This forms a very loose loop on the hook.

4 Pull both yarn ends gently to tighten the loop around the crochet hook shank.

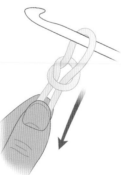

5 Make sure the loop is not TOO tight. It needs to slip easily along the shank.

Chain stitches
(abbreviated ch)

Chains are the basis of all crochet. This is the stitch you have to practice first because you need to make a length of chains to be able to make the first row or round of any other stitch. Practicing these will also give you the chance to get used to holding the hook and the yarn correctly.

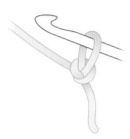

1 Start with the tip of the hook pointed upward, with the slip knot on your hook sitting loosely so there is enough gap to pull a strand of yarn through the loop on the hook.

2 Catch the yarn with the hook, circling it around the strand of yarn.

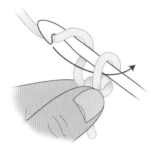

3 As you catch the yarn, turn the tip of the hook downward, holding the knot immediately under the loop on the hook with your left hand between your finger and thumb.

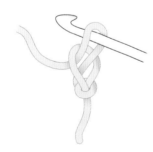

4 Then gently pull the strand of yarn through the loop on the hook. As soon as the tip of the hook comes through the loop, turn the tip of the hook immediately upward.

Chain space
[abbreviated ch sp]

1 A chain space is the space that has been made under a chain in the previous round or row and falls in between other stitches.

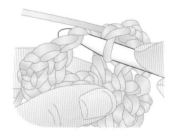

2 Stitches into a chain space are made directly into the hole created under the chain and not into the chain stitches themselves.

Slip stitch
(abbreviated ss)

A slip stitch is the shortest crochet stitch and is usually worked into other stitches rather than into a foundation chain, because it is rarely used to make a whole piece of crochet. It is mainly used to join rounds or to take the yarn neatly along the tops of stitches to get to a certain point without having to fasten off. It can also be used as a joining stitch.

1 To make a slip stitch, first insert the hook through the stitch (chain or chain space). Then wrap the yarn over the hook.

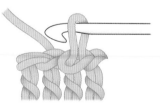

2 Pull the yarn through both the stitch (chain or chain space) and the loop on the hook at the same time, so you will be left with one loop on the hook.

Single crochet
(abbreviated sc)

Single crochet is the most commonly used stitch of all. It makes a firm tight crochet fabric. If you are just starting out, it is the best stitch to start with because it is the easiest to make.

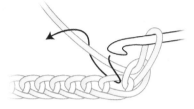

1 Make a foundation chain, then insert the tip of the hook into the 2nd chain from the hook. Catch the yarn with the hook by taking the hook around the back of the yarn strand. Pull the yarn through the chain only, with the hook pointed downward. As soon as you have brought the yarn through, immediately turn the hook upward—this will help to keep the loop on the hook and prevent it sliding off. Keep the hook in a horizontal position.

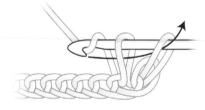

2 You will now have two loops on the hook. Wrap the yarn over the hook again (with the hook sitting at the front of the yarn), turn the hook to face downward and pull the yarn through the two loops, turning the hook to point upward as soon as you have pulled the yarn through.

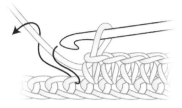

3 One loop is now left on the hook. Keep the hook pointed upward (this is the default position of the hook until you start the next stitch). Continue working one single crochet into each chain to the end of the foundation chain.

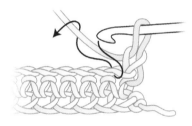

4 Turn the work to begin the next row. Make one chain and work the first single crochet into the top of the first single crochet in the row below (picking up the two loops at the top of the stitch). Work one single crochet into each single crochet stitch in the row below, to the end of the row.

5 For all subsequent rows, repeat Step 4.

Half double crochet
(abbreviated hdc)

Half doubles are stitches that are the next height up from a single crochet stitch. The yarn is wrapped over the hook first before going into the stitch (or space) and then once pulled through the stitch (or space) there will be three loops on the hook. The middle loop is from the strand that was wrapped over the hook. Before you attempt to pull the yarn through all three stitches, make sure the loops sit straight and loosely on the hook so that you can pull another strand through to complete the stitch.

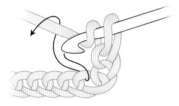

1 Make your foundation chain as usual to start. Before inserting the hook into the work, wrap the yarn over the hook. Then with the yarn wrapped over the hook, insert the hook through the 3rd chain from the hook. Work "yarn over hook" again (as shown by the arrow).

2 Pull the yarn through the chain. You now have three loops on the hook. Yarn over hook again and pull it through all three loops on the hook.

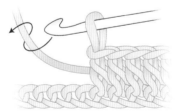

3 You will be left with one loop on the hook. Continue working one half double crochet into each chain to the end of the foundation chain.

first half double of row

4 Turn the work to begin the next row. Make two chains. Work one half double crochet into each half double stitch in the row below to the end of the row.

5 For all subsequent rows, repeat Step 4.

Double crochet
(abbreviated dc)

A double crochet is a very common stitch; it gives a more open fabric than a single crochet or a half double crochet, which both give a denser fabric, and it's one step taller than a half double crochet. As with the half double stitch, the yarn is wrapped over the hook before going into the stitch (or space) and then, once pulled through the stitch, there will be three loops on the hook. The middle loop is from the strand that was wrapped over the hook. Before you attempt to pull the yarn through the next two stitches on the hook, make sure the loops sit straight and loosely on the hook so you will be able to pull another strand through to complete the stitch.

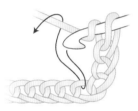

1 Before inserting the hook into the work, wrap the yarn over the hook. Then with the yarn wrapped over the hook, insert the hook through the 4th chain from the hook. Work "yarn over hook" again (as shown by the arrow).

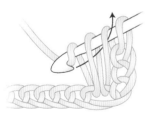

2 Pull the yarn through the chain. You now have three loops on the hook. Yarn over hook again and pull it through the first two loops on the hook.

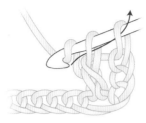

3 You now have two loops on the hook. Yarn round hook again and pull it through the two remaining loops.

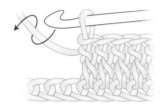

4 You will be left with one loop on the hook. Continue working one double crochet into each chain to the end of the foundation chain.

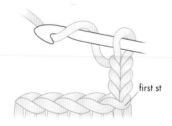

first st

5 Turn the work to begin the next row. Make three chains. Work one double crochet into each double crochet in the row below to the end of the row.

6 For all subsequent rows, repeat Step 5.

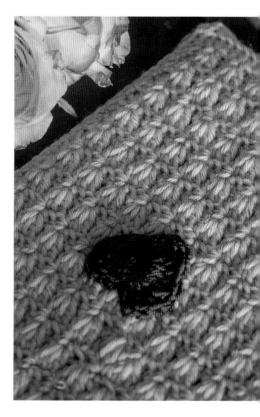

Treble
(abbreviated tr)

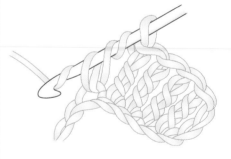

Yarn over hook twice, insert hook into the stitch, yarn over hook, pull a loop through (four loops on hook), yarn over hook, pull the yarn through two stitches (three loops on hook), yarn over hook, pull a loop through the next two stitches (two loops on hook), yarn over hook, pull a loop through the last two stitches.

Where to insert the hook in your crochet

One of the tricks of learning how to crochet is to understand clearly where to insert the hook to make a stitch, whether into a chain, a space in the crochet or into stitches in the row or round below.

The general rule for working into the stitch below to make a new stitch is to pick up both the top loops of the stitch—that means you will usually be inserting your hook under the two loops at the top of the stitch that look like a "V." However, you may be instructed in the pattern to pick up either only the front or only the back loop of the stitch, which gives the crochet a different "look" or texture.

Working into top of stitch

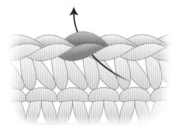

Unless otherwise directed the hook will be inserted into a stitch under both of the two loops on the top of the stitch. This is the standard technique.

Working into front loop of top of stitch

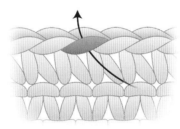

To pick up the front loop of the stitch, pick up the front loop from underneath at the front of the work.

Working into back loop of top of stitch

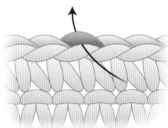

To pick up the back loop of the stitch, insert the hook between the front and the back loop, picking up the back loop from the front of the work.

Increasing

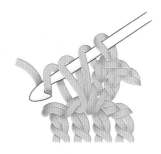

You can increase by working two or three stitches into one stitch or space from the previous row. The illustration shows a two-stitch increase being made using double crochet.

Decreasing

You can decrease by missing the next stitch and continuing to crochet, or by crocheting two or more stitches together. The basic technique for crocheting stitches together is the same for all stitches. The following example shows single crochet 2 stitches together (sc2tog).

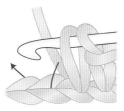

1 Insert the hook into the work, yarn over hook and pull through the work (two loops on hook), insert the hook in the next stitch, yarn over hook and pull the yarn through.

2 Yarn over hook again and pull through all three loops on the hook. You will then have one loop on the hook.

Cluster

Yarn over hook, insert hook into next stitch, pull yarn through work, yarn over hook, insert hook into same stitch, pull yarn through work, yarn over hook, insert hook into same stitch, pull yarn through work. Pull yarn through all seven loops on hook, 1 chain.

Adjusting the size of your cozy

If you want to increase the width of your project so it fits your own device, then you need to make more chains at the beginning of your work. The amount of chains will depend on the amount of stitches needed in the sequence of the pattern. These stitches are called "multiples" and the stitch multiple is given on the patterns in this book where it is relevant. Some patterns have been made specifically to fit the project, e.g. the egg cosies.

In the multiples you will see, for example: 4 sts + 3 sts (+ 1 for the base chain). The 4 sts is the sequence of the pattern, so stitches in the width you want have to be divisible by 4 (i.e. 24 sts), then you need to add an extra 3 sts, which could be for

end stitches. If you are starting from the beginning and you are instructed to make a foundation chain (base chain) then add the stitches in brackets. If you are not instructed to do this, then simply follow the multiples given exactly.

Simply add more rows to increase the length, but always finish on the Row/Round number as instructed.

Threading beads onto yarn

All the beads must be threaded onto the yarn before you start crocheting. If you run out of beads and need to add more, you will need to cut the yarn at the end of the row/round and thread more beads onto the ball and then join in the yarn again to continue. The size of the hole in the bead is usually too small for a yarn sewing needle eye to go through, and the yarn is too thick to be threaded onto a normal sewing needle, so here is a technique to thread the beads onto the yarn.

1 Make a loop with some cotton sewing thread and thread a sewing needle with the loop (not the end). Leave the loop hanging approx. 1in. (2.5cm) from the eye of the needle. Pull the yarn end through the loop of thread.

2 Thread the beads (two or three at a time), onto the sewing needle, pushing them down onto the strand of the yarn. Continue to thread beads until the required number is reached.

Beads are placed when working with the wrong side of the work facing you. The beads will sit at the back of the work, and so appear on the front (right side).

Placing a bead

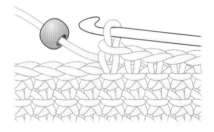

1 When a bead is needed, slide it up the strand toward the back of the work so it's ready to place in the right part of the stitch you're working.

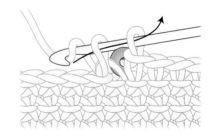

2 Work the stitch as indicated in the pattern. This will secure the bead at the back.

decorative stitches

These are the lovely—but not difficult to work—embroidery stitches used on some of the projects. If you've not worked a stitch before, practice on a scrap of fabric before starting to embroider a cozy.

Feather stitch

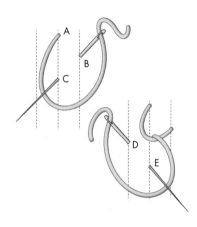

Bring the needle up at A, down at B, and up at C, looping the thread under the needle tip. (The distances between A and B and B and C should be the same.)

Take the needle down at D and up at E, again looping the thread under the needle tip. Continue working stitches alternately left and right.

Chain stitch

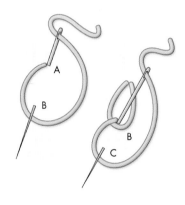

Bring the needle up at A, then loop the thread and insert the needle at A again. Bring it up at B, looping the thread under the needle tip. Pull the thread through.

Insert the needle at B and bring it up at C, again looping the thread under the needle tip. Continue, keeping all the stitches the same length. To anchor the last stitch in the chain, take the needle down just outside the loop, forming a little bar or "tie."

Lazy daisy stitch

Work as for chain stitch (see left), bringing the needle up inside the loop. To finish off the stitch, take the needle down just outside the loop, forming a little bar or "tie." You can work these stitches singly to form "leaves," or around in a circle to form a daisy-like "flower."

French knot

Bring the needle up from the back to the front. Wrap the thread two or three times around the tip of the needle, then reinsert the needle at the point where it first emerged, holding the wrapped threads with the thumbnail of your non-stitching hand. Pull the needle slowly and carefully through the wraps to form a small knot on the surface.

Bullion knot

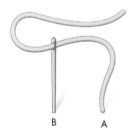

This is similar to a French knot, but creates a longer coil of thread rather than a single knot. Bring the needle up at A and take it down at B, leaving a loose loop of thread—the distance from A to B being the length of knot that you require. Bring the needle back up at A and wrap the thread around the needle five to eight times, depending on how long you want the knot to be. Hold the wrapped thread in place with your left hand and pull the needle all the way through. Insert the needle at B and pull through, easing the coiled stitches neatly into position.

Buttonhole wheels

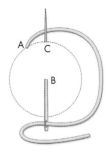

1 Using the circle as the stitch line, bring the needle out through A. Take the needle in through the center point B, and out through C. Keep the thread behind the needle and pull it out.

2 Continue with this process all around the circle. You can make solid circles by sewing each stitch very close together.

3 A finished buttonhole wheel looks like this.

lining crochet pieces

Method 1

1 Press and block the crochet piece, then measure it. Press the lining to make sure there are no creases. Cut out the fabric lining to fit the crocheted piece, allowing an extra 1in. (2.5cm) around each edge for hems. For example, if the crocheted piece measures 11 x 8½in. (28 x 21.5cm), cut out a piece of fabric 13 x 10½in. (33 x 26.5cm).

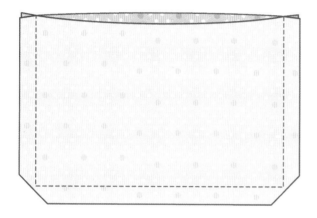

2 Place the two lining pieces with RS together. Pin and sew the side seams, and the bottom seam is there is one, ensuring that the lining is exactly the same measurement, at the sides, as the crochet piece. Trim across the corners. Do not turn RS out.

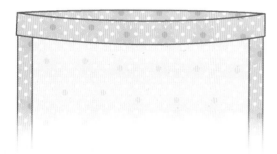

3 Fold the top edge of lining to the outside by 1in. (2.5cm) and press in place.

4 Make up the crochet piece and turn RS out. Insert the lining into the crochet piece, so WS are together. Ease the lining right down inside the crochet piece, so it fits nicely at the bottom. Using long plastic or glass-headed pins, pin the lining to the crochet piece around the opening; start pinning at the side seams, then pin the center (half way) of each side, then pin in between the center pin and the side seam pin. Add more pins if necessary to ensure it's neatly pinned all round.

5 If adding a ribbon tie, cut the ribbon in half or to the desired length. Insert one end of the ribbon at the center top in between the lining and the crochet piece—you may need to take out a pin to do this. Pin the ribbon in position and repeat on the other side.

6 Using a sewing needle and thread, slip stitch the lining and crochet piece together along the top edge, securing the ribbon at the same time, if adding. Trim the ends of the ribbon to neaten the edges if necessary.

7 Add two or three hand stitches in sewing thread on each side of the bottom edges to secure the lining to the crochet piece and keep it in position.

Method 2

If the crocheted piece must be lined before it is made up (particularly if it has a flap), follow Step 1 (above left) but allow only ½in. (1cm) extra around each edge for the seams. Place the lining on top of the crocheted piece with WS together. Then fold the lining piece ½in. (1cm) over to the WS all round and pin the folded edge to the crochet. Using a sewing needle and thread, sew the lining to the crocheted piece with hand stitches. Fold the crochet piece with RS together or as instructed in the pattern, then sew the seams of the crocheted piece using yarn and a yarn sewing needle. Turn RS out.

chapter one

cozy tech

striped wave iPad cover

We all love our iPads and you'll love yours even more with its own unique cover. The stripes and waves look bright and cheerful and you can fit the iPad inside either with or without its hard cover.

materials

Louisa Harding Cassia, 75% superwash wool/25% nylon light worsted (DK) weight yarn

1 x 1¾oz (50g) ball—approx. 144yd (132m)—each of:

A: 102 Ecru (off white)
B: 115 Lipstick (pink)
C: 108 Lime (green)

US size E/4 (3.5mm) crochet hook

40in. (1m) of ⁵⁄₁₆in. (7mm) wide ribbon

13 x 10½in. (33 x 26.5cm) of cotton lining fabric, allowing for an approx. 1in. (2.5cm) seam allowance on all sides

Hand sewing needle and thread to match lining

gauge

23 sts x 9 rows over a 4in. (10cm) square, working Wave pattern using US size E/4 (3.5mm) hook and Louisa Harding Cassia yarn.

finished measurement

Approx. 11 x 8½in. (28 x 21.5cm), to fit a standard iPad

note

The multiple is 10 sts + 3 sts (see page 18).

abbreviations

approx. approximate(ly)
ch chain
cont continu(e)(ing)
dc double crochet
dc3tog double crochet 3 stitches together
hdc half double crochet
rep repeat
RS right side
sc single crochet
st(s) stitch(es)
ss slip stitch
WS wrong side
yoh yarn over hook

colorway

Work the cover in a repeating stripe sequence of 2 rows A, 2 rows B, 2 rows C.

• •

cover

(made in one piece)
Foundation chain: Using A, make 43ch.
Row 1: Cont with A, 1dc in third ch from hook, 1dc in each of next 3 ch, dc3tog over next 3 ch, 1dc in each of next 3 ch, *3dc in next ch, 1dc in each of next 3 ch, dc3tog over next 3 ch, 1dc in each of next 3 ch; rep from * to last ch, 2dc in last ch.

tips

Make sure that you go into the first st at the beginning and end of the rows, and make the 2 double crochets into the top of the 3rd chain from the previous row.

When at the end of each 2-row color sequence, cut off the yarn but do not fasten off, then join in new color.

Row 2: Cont in color sequence, 3ch, 1dc in each of first 4 sts, dc3tog over next 3 sts, 1dc in each of next 3 sts, *3dc in next st, 1dc in each of next 3 sts, dc3tog over next 3 sts, 1dc in each of next 3 sts; rep from * to end, 2dc in top of 3-ch at end of row. Rep Row 2, changing color every 2 rows until work measures approx. 11in. (28cm). Fasten off.

edging 1:
Cont with same color, 1ch, 1sc in first st, 1sc in next st, [1hdc in each of next 2 sts, 1dc in each of next 3 sts, 1hdc in each of next 2 sts, 1sc in each of next 3 sts] four times. Fasten off.

edging 2:
Working on underside of Foundation chain, join A on RS in top of last double crochet at start of Row 1.
3ch, 1dc in first ch, [1hdc in each of next 2 ch, 1sc in each of next 3 ch, 1hdc in each of next 2 ch, 1dc in each of next 3 ch] four times. Fasten off.

finishing

Block Cover if necessary and sew in ends.
With RS together, join side and bottom seams.

Make and insert lining and ribbon for ties at top edge, following instructions on page 22, Method 1.

key

⬭	**ch** chain
	dc double crochet
	dc3tog double crochet 3 stitches together
	3dc 3 double crochet stitches in one stitch
▶	starting pointer
◁	ending pointer

wave stitch chart

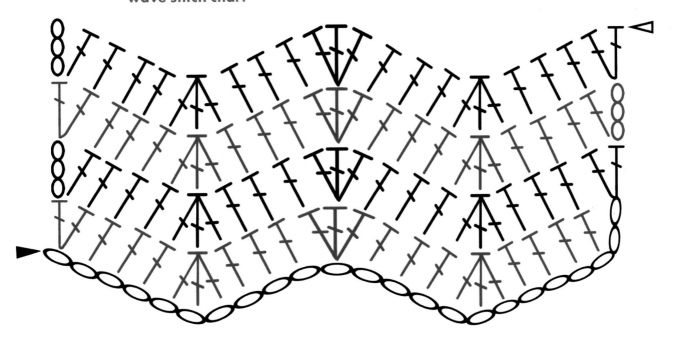

cell phone cozies

This is a great project for a beginner; quick to make using a basic single crochet stitch and decorated with a picot edge and flower. It makes a really great gift and can be made in no time, and for any size cell phone.

materials

Louisa Harding Cassia, 75% superwash wool/25% nylon light worsted (DK) weight yarn
1 x 1¾oz (50g) ball—approx. 144yd (132m)—each of:

cozy
A: 103 Chick (yellow)
     105 Glacier (pale blue)
     104 Powder (pale pink)
     112 Prince (dark blue)

flowers
B: 115 Lipstick (bright pink)

french knot
C: 102 Ecru (off white)

US size D/3 (3mm) crochet hook

US size E/4 (3.5mm) crochet hook

gauge

20 sts x 22 rows over 4in. (10cm) square, working single crochet using US size E/4 (3.5mm) hook and Louisa Harding Cassia yarn.

finished measurement

Approx. 5in. (12.5cm) long x 2¾in. (7cm) wide, to fit an iPhone 5 measuring 5in. (12.5cm) long x 2¼in. (6cm) wide

note

The multiple is any number of sts (+ 1 for the base ch) (see page 18).

abbreviations

approx. approximate(ly)
ch chain
rep repeat
RS right side
sc single crochet
st(s) stitch(es)
ss slip stitch
WS wrong side

cozy

Row 1: Using US size E/4 (3.5mm) crochet hook and A, make 15ch, 1sc in second ch from hook, 1sc in each ch to end. (14 sts)
Row 2: 1ch, 1sc in each st. (14 sts)
Rep Row 2 until work measures approx. 10in. (25.5cm)—55 rows, or twice length of device—finishing with a WS row. Do not fasten off.

picot edge:

Next row (RS): *3ch, ss in first of 3-ch, miss next st, 1sc in each of next 2 sts; rep from * to end, ending last repeat with 1sc in last 2 sts, 3ch, ss in first of 3-ch, miss next st, 1sc in last st. (5 picots)
Fasten off.
Join yarn on RS at other end of piece (start of Row 1). Working on underside of foundation ch, *3ch, ss in first of 3-ch, miss next ch, 1sc in each of next 2 ch; rep from * to end, ending last rep with 1sc in last 2-ch, 3ch, ss in first of 3-ch, miss next st, 1sc in last ch. (5 picots).
Fasten off.

flowers

(make 1 per Cozy)
Using US size D/3 (3mm) crochet hook and B, make 4ch, join with a ss in first ch to form a ring.
Round 1 (RS): [5ch, 1ss in ring] 5 times. (5 petals)
Fasten off.
Using C, make a French knot in the center.

finishing

Fold Cozy lengthways with RS together. Pin and sew side seams.
Block and press.
Turn RS out.
Sew Flower onto center on RS of Cozy.

patchwork laptop cover

A great piece of patchwork to show off and protect your laptop—make as many squares as you need to cover the size. Here I've used the colors in Debbie Bliss Baby Cashmerino, because the shades are very on-trend and it feels very soft to carry around.

materials

Debbie Bliss Baby Cashmerino, 55% wool/33% acrylic/12% cashmere sport weight (lightweight DK) yarn 1¾oz (50g) balls—approx. 137yd (125m) per ball—of:

squares
1 ball each of:
700 Ruby (red)
202 Light blue (pale blue)
94 Rose pink (pale pink)
03 Mint (pale green)
84 Toffee (bronze)
91 Acid yellow (yellow)
101 Ecru (off white)
65 Clotted cream (cream)
204 Baby blue (mid blue)
57 Mist (gray)

top edging
1 ball of:
202 Light Blue (pale blue)

US size C/2 (2.5mm) crochet hook—or size needed to make a 1¾in. (4.5cm) square

2 pieces of lining fabric, each approx. 18 x 14in. (45 x 35cm)

1yd (1m) of 1in. (2.5cm) wide ribbon

Large snap fastener approx. ¾in. (2cm) diameter

gauge

Each square measures approx. 1¾in.(4.5cm).

finished measurement

Approx. 15¾in. (40cm) wide x 12in. (30cm) long, to fit a Macbook Pro measuring 14½in. (36.5cm) wide x 10in. (25cm) long x ½in. (1cm) deep

abbreviations

alt alternate
approx. approximate(ly)
ch chain
dc double crochet
foll following
hdc half double crochet
rep repeat
RS right side
sc single crochet
sp space
ss slip stitch
st(s) stitches

colorway

Make total of 126 squares in the following colors:
Red x 14
Pale blue x 14
Pale pink x 14
Pale green x 14
Bronze x 14
Yellow x 14
Off white x 13
Cream x 12
Mid blue x 10
Gray x 7

square

Make 4ch, join with a ss to form a ring.

Round 1 (RS): 1ch, 12sc in ring, join with a ss in first sc. (12 sts)

Round 2: 3ch (counts as first dc), 1dc in same st, 2dc in each st to end, join with a ss in first dc. (24 sts)

Round 3: 3ch (counts as 1dc), 2dc in same st (first corner), 1hdc in next st, 1sc in each of next 3 sts, 1hdc in next st. *3dc in next st (second corner), 1hdc in next st, 1sc in each of next 3 sts, 1hdc in next st; rep from * twice more (four corners), join with a ss in top of first 3-ch. Fasten off.

finishing

Block and press Squares.

Set out Front with 9 Squares across (width) x 7 down (length), with the colors evenly spaced and with squares RS facing up.

Join in strips with RS together, first vertically then horizontally, using a neutral color yarn. Press.

Rep for back.

With RS together, join sides and bottom seams of front and back, leaving top open. Turn RS out.

top edging

With RS facing, join A in a st to side of one seam. 1ch, 1sc in same st, 1sc in next and each st around top to end, join with a ss in first sc.

Fasten off.

Make and insert lining following instructions on page 22, Method 1. Attach edging ribbon at top edge of lining before slip stitching crochet and lining together.

kindle cozy

This Kindle cozy is made using a bobble stitch, which makes a lovely texture and gives a good thickness to keep the Kindle protected. Here I've used a lovely Dorset button to match the yarn color and lining.

materials

Debbie Bliss Baby Cashmerino, 55% wool/33% acrylic/ 12% cashmere sport weight (lightweight DK) yarn
2 x 1¾oz (50g) balls—approx. 274yd (250m) of:
68 Peach Melba

US size D/3 (3mm) crochet hook

Approx. 10¼in. (25.5cm) square of cotton lining fabric

Sewing needle and thread

Button

Snap fastener

gauge

Approx. 9 bobbles x 10 bobble rows over 4in. (10cm) square, using US size D/3 (3mm) hook and Debbie Bliss Baby Cashmerino.

finished measurement

To fit a Kindle 6¾ x 4½ x ½in. (17 x 11.5 x 1.5cm), cozy measures approx. 7½ x 5¾in. (19 x 14.75cm)

note

The multiple is 4 sts + 3 sts (+ 1 for the base ch) (see page 18).

abbreviations

approx. approximate(ly)
ch chain
dc double crochet
rep repeat
RS right side
sc single crochet
ss slip stitch
st(s) stitch(es)
WS wrong side
yoh yarn over hook

special abbreviation

5dcCL 5 double crochet cluster/bobble—yoh, insert hook in st, yoh, pull yarn through work (3 loops on hook). Yoh, pull yarn through first 2 loops on hook (2 loops on hook). Yoh, insert hook in same st, yoh, pull yarn through work (4 loops on hook), yoh, pull yarn through first 2 loops on hook (3 loops left on hook). Yoh, insert hook in same st, yoh, pull yarn through work (5 loops on hook), yoh, pull yarn through first 2 loops on hook (4 loops left on hook). Yoh, insert hook in same st, yoh, pull yarn through work (6 loops on hook), yoh, pull yarn through first 2 loops on hook (5 loops left on hook). Yoh, insert hook in same st, yoh, pull yarn through work (7 loops on hook), yoh, pull yarn through first 2 loops on hook (6 loops left on hook). Yoh, pull yarn through all 6 loops on hook (1 loop left on hook). Make 1ch to complete 5dcCL.

tip
When working a single crochet into the top of the 5-double crochet cluster, make the single crochet stitch into the chain at the top of the cluster.

main piece

Row 1 (RS): Make 28ch, 1sc in second ch from hook, 1sc in each ch to end. (27 sts)

Begin bobble pattern

Row 2 (WS): 1ch, *1sc in each of first 3 sc, 5dcCL in next sc; rep from * to last 3 sts, 1sc in each of last 3 sc. (6 bobbles)

Row 3: 1ch, *1sc in each of next 3 sc, 1sc in top of next 5dcCL; rep from * to last 3 sts, 1sc in each of last 3 sc.

Row 4: 1ch, 1sc in first sc, 5dcCL in next sc, *1sc in each of next 3 sc, 5dcCL in next sc; rep from * to last st, 1sc in last sc. (7 bobbles)

Row 5: 1ch, 1sc in first sc, *1sc in top of next 5dcCL, 1sc in each of next 3 sc; rep from * to last 5dcCL, 1sc in top of last 5dcCL, 1sc in last sc.

Rep Rows 2–5 until 37 bobble rows have been worked or work measures approx. 15in. (38cm) ending on a Row 5.

Fasten off.

tab

Row 1: Make 8ch, 1sc in second ch from hook, 1sc in each ch to end. (7 sts)

Row 2: 1ch, 1sc in each st to end. (7 sts)

Rep Row 2 until tab measures approx. 3½in. (9cm). Fasten off.

finishing

Pin and block Tab.

With RS together join side seams of Main Piece, leaving top open. Turn RS out.

Make and insert lining for the Main Piece (see page 22, Method 1), and line the Tab following Method 2. Pin along top edge of Main Piece and insert Tab between lining and crochet piece, with WS of Tab facing WS of lining, approx. 1in. (2.5cm) down into lining on one side only. Hand sew lining to crochet piece using cotton thread around top of lining, incorporating one end of Tab.

Sew button onto RS of Tab at end that flaps over onto other side of crochet piece. Sew one side of snap fastener to Tab lining underneath button. Sew other side of snap fastener onto main crochet piece to match.

iPod cozy

A pretty drawstring cozy to pop onto your iPod to protect it while it's in your purse, made using a fingering (4ply) yarn with a pretty lace edging.

materials

Fyberspates Scrumptious 4ply, 55% superwash merino wool, 45% silk fingering (4ply) yarn
1 x 3½oz (100g) hank—approx. 399yd (365m)—of
A: 318 Glisten (pale gray)

Debbie Bliss Rialto Lace, 100% extra fine merino laceweight yarn
1 x 1¾oz (50g) ball—approx. 427yd (390m)—of:
B: 035 Acid Yellow (yellow-green)

US size C/2 (2.5mm) crochet hook

Approx. 20in. (50cm) of ¼in. (5mm) wide ribbon

gauge

Approx. 26 sts x 32 rows over 4in. (10cm) square working single crochet using US size C/2 (2.5mm) hook and Fyberspates Scrumptious 4ply yarn.

finished measurement

To fit an iPod Touch, approx: 5in. (13cm) high, 2⅜in. (6cm) wide

note

The multiple for the cosy is any number of sts (+ 1 for the base ch). The multiple for the edging is 12 sts + 2 sts (see page 18).

abbreviations

approx. approximate(ly)
ch chain
ch sp chain space
dc double crochet
rep repeat
RS right side
sc single crochet
sp space
st(s) stitch(es)
WS wrong side

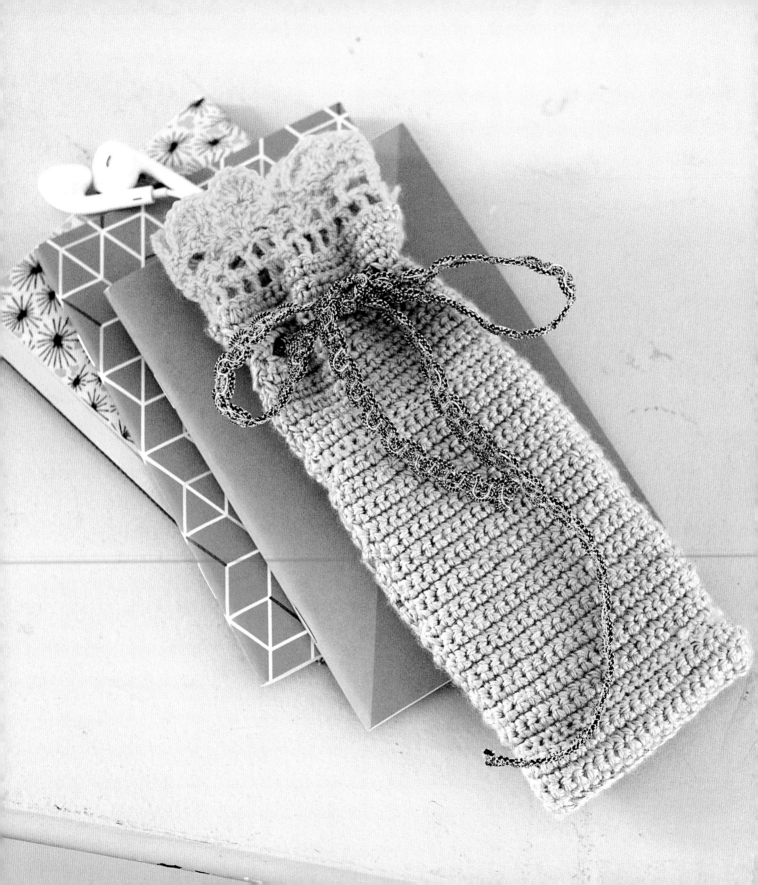

cozy

(make two, Front and Back)

Row 1: Using A, make 21ch, 1sc in second ch from hook, 1sc in each ch to end. (20 sts)

Rows 2–4: 1ch, 1sc in each st to end. (20 sts)

Cut yarn, do not fasten off.

Rows 5–6: Join B, 1ch, 1sc in each st to end. (20 sts)

Cut yarn, do not fasten off.

Row 7: Join A, 1ch, 1sc in each st to end. (20 sts)

Rep Row 7 until work measures 4½in. (11.5cm), ending on a WS Row.

Cut yarn, do not fasten off.

Next 2 rows: Join B, 1ch, 1sc in each st to end. (20 sts)

Next 11 rows: Join A, 1ch, 1sc in each st to end.

make ribbon holes:

Next row: 1ch, 1sc in first st, 2ch, miss next 2 sts, *1sc in each of next 2 sts, 2ch, miss next 2 sts; rep from * to end, 1sc in last st.

Next row: 1ch, 2sc in first st, 2sc in next ch sp, *1sc in each of next 2 sts, 2sc in next ch sp; rep from * to last st, 2sc in last st. (22 sts)

Next 2 Rows: 1ch, 1sc in each st to end. (22 sts)

Next Row: 1ch, 2sc in first st, 1sc in each st to last st, 2sc in last st. (24 sts)

Cut yarn, do not fasten off.

edging:

Row 1 (RS): Join B, 3ch (counts as 1dc), 1dc in first st, 1ch, *miss next st, [1dc, 1ch] in next st; rep from * to last 2 sts, 1dc in each of last 2 sts. (14 dc)

Row 2:

1ch, 1sc in first st,

2ch, [miss next dc, next ch sp], 1dc in next dc,

2ch, [miss next ch sp, next dc], 1dc in next ch sp,

2ch, [miss next dc, next ch sp], 1dc in next dc,

2ch, [miss next ch sp, next dc], 1sc in next ch sp,

2ch, [miss next dc, next ch sp], 1dc in next dc,

2ch, [miss next ch sp, next dc], 1dc in next ch sp,

2ch, [miss next dc, next ch sp], 1dc in next dc,

2ch, [miss next ch sp, next dc], 1sc in top of 3-ch from previous row.

Row 3:

1ch, 1sc in first st,

2ch, miss next ch sp, 1sc in next st,

2ch, miss next ch sp, [1dc, 1ch in next st] twice, 1dc in same st, [2ch, miss next ch sp, 1sc in next st] three times,

2ch, miss next ch sp, [1dc, 1ch in next st] twice, 1dc in same st,

2ch, miss next ch sp, 1sc in next st,

2ch, miss next ch sp, 1sc in last st.

Row 4:

4ch, [miss first ch sp, miss next sc, miss next ch sp], 1dc in next dc,

3dc in next ch sp, 1ch, miss next dc,

3dc in next ch sp, 1dc in next dc,

1ch, [miss next ch sp, miss next sc, miss next ch sp], 1dc in next sc, 1ch,

[miss next ch sp, miss next sc, miss next ch sp], 1dc in next dc,

3dc in next ch sp, 1ch, miss next dc,

3dc in next ch sp, 1dc in next dc,

[miss next ch sp, miss next sc, miss next ch sp],

1dc in last sc.

Row 5:

1ch, miss first dc, 1sc in next dc,

miss next dc, 7dc in next dc, miss next dc, 1sc in next ch sp,

miss next dc, 7dc in next dc, miss next dc, 1sc in next dc,

miss next ch sp, 7dc in next dc,

miss next ch sp, 1sc in next dc,

miss next dc, 7dc in next dc,

miss next dc, 1sc in next ch sp,

miss next dc, 7dc in next dc,

miss next dc, 1sc in next dc, 1sc in 3rd of 4-ch.

Fasten off.

finishing

With RS together join side and bottom seams.

Thread ribbon through ribbon holes and pull ribbon to close once iPod is inside.

striped laptop cozy

This is made using puff stitch, a lovely thick stitch that will keep the laptop protected. It's very colorful, with bright stripes and a ribbon tie.

materials

Louisa Harding Cassia, 75% superwash wool/25% nylon light worsted (DK) weight yarn

1 x 1¾oz (50g) ball—approx. 144yd (132m)—each of:

A: 112 Prince (mid blue)
B: 108 Lime (green)
C: 104 Powder (pale pink)
D: 111 Earth (brown)
E: 103 Chick (yellow)
F: 105 Glacier (pale blue)
G: 115 Lipstick (bright pink)
H: 101 White (white)

US size E/4 (3.5mm) crochet hook

Piece of cotton lining fabric size of laptop, plus ⅝in. (1.5cm) all round for top, side and bottom seams.

Approx. 1yd (1m) pink ribbon

gauge

10 Puff stitches and 8 rows over 4in. (10cm) square, using US size E/4 (3.5mm) hook and Louisa Harding Cassia yarn.

finished measurement

Approx. 13in. (33cm) wide x 10½in. (27cm) long, to fit a Macbook Air measuring 12in. (30cm) wide x 7½in. (19cm) long.

abbreviations

approx. approximate(ly)
ch chain
cont continu(e)(ing)
dc double crochet
rep repeat
RS right side
sc single crochet
sp space
ss slip stitch
sp space
st(s) stitch(es)
yoh yarn over hook

special abbreviation

3dc-Puff 3 double crochet puff stitch—[yoh and insert hook into st, yoh and pull loop up to dc height] three times, yoh, pull through all loops on hook.

note

The multiple is 4 sts + 3 sts (+ 1 for the base ch) (see page 18).

cozy

Using A, make 72ch.

Row 1: 1sc in second ch from hook, 1sc in each ch to end. (71 sts)

Rows 2–3: 1ch, 1sc in each st to end. (71 sts)

Row 4: 1ch, 1sc in first st, [3dc-Puff, 2ch, 3dc-Puff] in next st, *miss 3 sts, [3dc-Puff, 2ch, 3dc-Puff] in next st; rep from * to last st, 1sc in last st.

Cut yarn A, do not fasten off.

Row 5: Join B, 1ch, 1sc in first st, [3dc-Puff, 2ch, 3dc-Puff] in first 2-ch sp, *miss 2 Puffs, [3dc-Puff, 2ch, 3dc-Puff] into next 2-ch sp; rep from * ending 1sc in last sc.

Cut yarn, do not fasten off.

Rep Row 5, changing colors in sequence A, B, C, D, E, F, G, H until approx. 10in. (25cm) or 24 Puff Rows have been worked, ending with A.

Do not fasten off.

top edge:

Next row: 1ch, 1sc in top of first Puff, 2sc in next 2-ch (in center of 2 Puffs), 1sc in top of next Puff, *1sc in top of next Puff, 2sc in next 2-ch, 1sc in top of next Puff; rep from * until end. (71 sts)

Next 2 rows: 1ch, 1sc in each st to end. (71 sts)

Fasten off.

finishing

Sew in ends. With RS together fold Cozy in half widthways and sew up side and bottom seams.

Make a lining incorporating ribbon ties (see page 22, Method 1). Insert lining into Cozy with WS together. Turn over the hem of the lining at the top edge and pin in place around the edge of the crochet piece. Hand sew edge in place.

iPad cozy with flap

A bright and cheerful iPad cozy that will hold an iPad in its hard cover and give it added protection. This makes a great gift for the man in your life.

materials

Debbie Bliss Rialto DK, 100% merino wool light worsted (DK) weight yarn
1 x 1¾oz (50g) ball—approx. 115yd (105m)—each of:
A: 70 Pool (blue)
C: 45 Gold (yellow)
D: 12 Scarlet (red)

Louisa Harding Cassia, 75% superwash wool/25% nylon light worsted (DK) weight yarn
1 x 1¾oz (50g) ball—approx. 144yd (132m)—of:
B: 113 Silver (gray)

US size E/4 (3.5mm) crochet hook

1 button

8 x 12in. (20 x 30cm) pieces x 2 of cotton lining fabric for the sides

8 x 8in. (20 x 20cm) piece of cotton lining fabric for the flap

Hand sewing needle and thread to match lining

gauge

21 sts x 22 rows over a 4in. (10cm) square, working single crochet using US size E/4 (3.5mm) hook and Debbie Bliss Rialto light worsted (DK) yarn.

finished measurement

Approx. 11 x 8in. (27.5 x 20cm), to fit a standard iPad in its hard cover

note

The multiple is any number of sts (+ 1 for the base ch) (see page 18).

abbreviations

approx. approximate(ly)
ch chain
rep repeat
RS right side
sc single crochet
sc2tog single crochet 2 stitches together
st(s) stitch(es)
ss slip stitch

• •

cozy

Made in one piece, starting at top edge of one side and finishing at top edge of other side.
Row 1 (RS): Using A, make 39ch, 1sc in second ch from hook, 1sc in each ch to end. (38 sts)
Next 4 Rows: 1ch, 1sc in each st to end. (38 sts)
Cut yarn, do not fasten off. Join B.
Next 17 Rows: Using B, 1sc in each st to end.
Cut yarn, do not fasten off. Join C.
Next 37 Rows: Using C, 1sc in each st to end.
Cut yarn, do not fasten off.
Next 8 Rows: Using A, 1sc in each st to end.
Cut yarn, do not fasten off.

Next 37 Rows: Using C, 1sc in each st to end.
Cut yarn, do not fasten off.
Next 17 Rows: Using B, 1sc in each st to end.
Cut yarn, do not fasten off.
Next 4 Rows: Using A, 1sc in each st to end.
Cut yarn, do not fasten off. Join D.

flap:
Rows 1–7: Using D, 1ch, 1sc in each st to end. (38 sts)
Row 8: 1ch, sc2tog, 1sc in each st to last 2 sts, sc2tog. (36 sts)
Rep last 2 rows until 18 sts remain, then rep Row 8 until 4 sts remain.
Next Row: [Sc2tog] twice. (2 sts)
Next Row: Sc2tog.
Do not fasten off.

button loop:
Make 8ch, join with a ss in top of last sc2tog.
Fasten off.

finishing

Sew in ends. Block and press.

Line crochet piece on WS (before sewing seams)—see page 22, Method 2 for lining instructions.

With RS together, fold bottom edge to match first row of Flap. Pin side seams and sew.
Turn RS out. Attach button on RS of front to match Button loop.

striped cell phone cozy

This cozy fits a larger cell phone, and is nice and bright and easy to find in a purse! Here I've used Baby Cashmerino yarn as I love the colors, but this is a perfect project for using up scraps as it requires very little yarn.

materials

Debbie Bliss Baby Cashmerino, 55% wool/33% acrylic/ 12% cashmere sport weight (lightweight DK) yarn
1 x 1¾oz (50g) ball–approx. 137yd (125m)–each of:

A: 68 Peach Melba (peach)
B: 59 Mallard (dark blue)
C: 02 Apple (light green)
D: 101 Ecru (off white)
E: 06 Candy Pink (pink)
F: 202 Light Blue (light blue)
G: 34 Red (red)
H: 90 Leaf (dark green)

US size D/3 (3mm) crochet hook

gauge

20 sts x 24 rows over a 4in. (10cm) square, working single crochet using US size D/3 (3mm) hook and Debbie Bliss Baby Cashmerino yarn.

finished measurement

Approx. 3½ x 6in. (9 x 15cm)

note

To fit a Samsung S5 cell phone, but you can make it any size. The multiple is any number of sts (+ 1 for the base ch) (see page 18).

abbreviations

approx. approximate(ly)
ch chain
dc double crochet
rep repeat
RS right side
sc single crochet
ss slip stitch
st(s) stitch(es)

cozy

This is made in one piece.
Make 1 row stripes using A, B, C, D, E, F, G, H, changing color on each row.
Row 1: Using any color make 21ch, 1sc in second ch from hook and each ch to end. (20 sts)
Cut yarn, do not fasten off.
Row 2: Join next color, 1ch, 1sc in each st to end. (20 sts)
Cut yarn, do not fasten off.
Repeat Row 2 until 72 rows have been worked or to required length.
Fasten off.
Sew in ends.

bow

(make one)
Using D, make 16ch, join with a ss to form a ring.
Round 1 (RS): 1ch (does not count as a st), 1sc in each ch to end, join with a ss in first sc. (16 sts)
Round 2: 3ch, (counts as dc), 1dc in each st to end; join with a ss in top of first 3-ch. (16 sts)
Round 3: 1ch, 1sc in each st to end, join with a ss in first sc.
Fasten off leaving a tail of approx. 17½in. (45cm).

finishing

With RS together fold Cozy in half lengthways and sew up side seams.
Block and press.

Turn Bow RS out and hold flat with fasten off st and tail at the top at the front center. Using yarn tail, wrap yarn around center of ring tightly to create bow shape, then secure in place on one side of cozy approx. 6 rows from the top, using a yarn sewing needle.

chapter two

cozy living

bunny egg cozies

These cute little egg cozies have bunny ears and are made using standard single crochet to fit an average-sized egg. They are made in a spiral so it's useful to use a stitch marker to mark the beginning and end of each round.

materials

Debbie Bliss Rialto DK, 100% merino wool light worsted (DK) weight yarn

1 x 1¾oz (50g) ball—approx. 115yd (105m)—each of:

A: 58 Grass (green)
B: 44 Aqua (blue)
C: 64 Mauve (pink)
D: 69 Citrus (yellow)

US size E/4 (3.5mm) crochet hook

Stitch marker

6 small pink beaded fabric bows

gauge

17 sts x 19 rows over a 4in. (10cm) square, working single crochet using US size E/4 (3.5mm) hook.

finished measurement

Approx. 1½in. (4cm) diameter

abbreviations

approx. approximate(ly)
ch chain
cont continu(e)(ing)
rep repeat
RS right side
sc single crochet
sc2tog single crochet 2 stitches together
st(s) stitch(es)
ss slip stitch
WS wrong side

. . . .

cozy

(make 1 each in A, B, C, and D)
Make 2ch, 6sc into second ch from hook.
Round 1 (RS): 2sc in each sc to end. (12 sc)
Cont in rounds with RS always facing.
Round 2: Rep Round 1. (24 sc)
Rounds 3–7: 1sc in each sc to end.
Round 8: *1sc in next sc, sc2tog over next 2 sc; rep from * to end. (16 sc)
Round 9: 1sc in each sc, join with a ss in first sc of round.
Fasten off.

ears

(make 2 per Cozy)
Row 1: Using A, B, C, or D, make 5ch, 1sc in second ch from hook, 1sc in each ch to end. (4 sts)
Rows 2–5: 1ch, 1sc in each st to end. (4 sts)
Row 6: 1ch, [sc2tog] twice. (2 sts)
Row 7: 1ch, 1sc in each st.
Row 8: 1ch, sc2tog.
Fasten off.

finishing

Sew in ends on WS and turn Cozy RS out.
Pin and block Ears.
Position and pin Ears onto top of RS of Cozy and sew in place.
Sew one bow onto the left-hand Ear.

floral tea cozy

This cozy is made using a "post" stitch, which gives the cozy an extra thickness to keep your tea nice and hot.

materials

cozy
Debbie Bliss Blue Faced Leicester Aran, 100% wool worsted (Aran) weight yarn
2 x 1¾oz (50g) balls—approx. 164yd (150m)—of:
MC: 21 Rose (pink)

flowers
Debbie Bliss Rialto DK, 100% merino wool light worsted (DK) weight yarn
1 x 1¾oz (50g) ball—approx. 115yd (105m)—each of:
A: 69 Citrus (yellow)
B: 02 Ecru (off white)

leaves
Debbie Bliss Blue Faced Leicester DK, 100% wool light worsted (DK) weight yarn
1 x 1¾oz (50g) ball—approx. 118yd (108m)—of:
C: 15 Sage (green)

US size E/4 (3.5mm) crochet hook

US size G/6 (4mm) crochet hook

US size J/10 (6mm) crochet hook

gauge

20 fpdc sts x 22 pattern rows over 4in. (10cm) square, using US size G/6 (4mm) hook and Debbie Bliss Blue Faced Leicester Aran yarn.

finished size

To fit standard sized 5-cup tea pot

abbreviations

ch chain
cont continue
dc double crochet
hdc half double crochet
MC main color
rep repeat
RS right side
sc single crochet
sc2tog single crochet 2 stitches together
sp space
ss slip stitch
st(s) stitch(es)
WS wrong side
yoh yarn over hook

special abbreviations

fpdc Front post double crochet (raised double crochet round front)—working on st from previous round, yoh and insert hook from front and around post (stem) of next dc from right to left. (When working at beginning of row, insert hook from back between last st or group of ch from previous row and next dc.) Yoh, pull yarn through work, yoh, pull yarn through first 2 loops on hook. Yoh, pull yarn through 2 loops on hook (1 loop on hook).

bpsc raised single crochet round back—working on st from previous round, insert hook from back and around post (stem) of next single crochet from right to left. Yoh, pull yarn through work, yoh, pull yarn through 2 loops on hook (1 loop on hook).

3dcCL 3 double crochet cluster—yoh, insert hook in st, yoh, pull yarn through work (3 loops on hook). Yoh, pull yarn through 2 loops on hook (2 loops on hook). Yoh, insert hook in same st, yoh, pull yarn through work (4 loops on hook). Yoh, pull yarn through 2 loops on hook (3 loops on hook). Yoh, insert hook in same st, yoh, pull yarn through work (5 loops on hook). Yoh, pull yarn through 2 loops on hook (4 loops on hook). Yoh, pull yarn through all 4 loops on hook (1 loop on hook).

● ●

main piece

(make 2, Front and Back)
Row 1 (RS): Using US size J/10 (6mm) crochet hook and MC, make 30ch loosely, 1dc in fourth ch from hook (counts as first dc), 1dc in each ch to end. (28 sts)
Row 2: 1ch, 1sc in each st to end.

Row 3: Change to US size G/6 (4mm) crochet hook. 3ch, miss first st, 1dc in next st, 1fpdc around first 3-ch from Row 1, *1dc in next st, 1fpdc around next dc from Row 1; rep from * to end, making last fpdc around last dc from Row 1. (26 fpdc)
Row 4: 1ch, miss first st, *1sc in top of first fpdc, miss 1dc, *1sc in top of next fpdc, miss 1dc; rep from * ending 1sc in top of first 3-ch of previous row.
Row 5: 3ch, miss first st, 1dc in next st, 1fpdc around first fpdc, 1dc in next st, *1fpdc around next fpdc, 1dc in next st; rep from * ending last rep with 1fpdc around last fpdc. (26 fpdc)
Rep Rows 4 and 5 until work measures 5½in. (14cm), ending on a Row 5.
Next row (decrease): Working into top of fpdc stitches only, *sc2tog, 1sc in each of next 2 sts; rep from * to last 2 sts, sc2tog. (19 sts)
Next row: 1ch, 1sc in each of next 3 sts, sc2tog, 1sc in each of next 4 sts, sc2tog, 1sc in each of next 3 sts, sc2tog, 1sc in each of last 3 sts. (16 sts)
Next row: 1ch, 1sc in each st to end. (16 sts)
Next row: 1ch, [sc2tog] to end. (8 sts)
Next row: 1ch, 1sc in each st to end. (8 sts)
Next row: 1ch, [sc2tog, 1sc in next st] twice, sc2tog. (5 sts)
Fasten off.

flower

(make 6)
Using US size E/4 (3.5mm) crochet hook and A, make 4ch, join with a ss in first ch to form a ring.
Work on RS throughout.
Round 1: 1ch, 12sc in ring. Break yarn, but do not fasten off. Join round with a ss in first sc using B.
Round 2: Cont using B, 1ch, 1sc in first st, 1sc in next st, *3ch, 3dcCL in same st, 3ch, 1sc in same st. 1sc in each of next 2 sts; rep

tip

Pin before sewing and try it on your teapot to check you have left big enough gaps for the handle and spout.

from * to end, ending last rep with 1sc in last st, ss in first sc of round. (6 petals)

Round 3: 1ch, *1sc/rb of same sc (between first two petals), 3ch, miss next petal. (Cont to work on RS, but flip next petal forward so chain sits at back of work); rep from * five times more, join last 3-ch with a ss in first 1-ch. (6 loops)

Round 4: Cont to work on RS, but make following sts in loops at back of petals made from previous round. 1ch, *[1sc, 1hdc, 5dc, 1hdc, 1sc] in next loop; rep from * five times more, join with a ss in first 1-ch. (6 petals)
Fasten off.

leaf

(make 7)
Make sts into Foundation chain, then make sts into underside of Foundation chain.
Using US size E/4 (3.5mm) crochet hook and C, make 8ch.

Round 1 (RS): 1sc in 2nd ch from hook, 1hdc in next ch, 1dc in each of next 2 ch, 2dc in next ch, 1hdc in next ch, 1sc in next ch, 2ch, turn work so bottom of foundation ch is at top and cont along bottom of sts just made, 1sc in first ch, 1hdc in next ch, 2dc in next ch, 1dc in each of next 2 ch, 1hdc in next ch, 1sc in last ch, join with a ss in first sc tip of leaf.
Fasten off.

finishing

Sew in ends.
With RS together sew side seams, leaving gaps for handle and spout. Using a wool sewing needle, weave around through hole at top of cozy and pull yarn tight to close hole.
Sew in end at tip of Leaf, leave end at base for sewing onto cozy.
Pin and block Leaves.

Working on RS, pin and sew one flower at top in center of cozy.
Pin and sew five Flowers evenly around top center. Pin and sew one Leaf in between each Flower and one Leaf on each side underneath top Flower.

hot water bottle cosy

This hot water bottle cosy makes a great gift and will cheer up the coldest of winter nights.

materials

Louisa Harding Cassia 75% superwash wool, 25% nylon light worste (DK) weight yarn

2 x 1¾oz (50g) balls—approx. 288yd (264m)—of:
MC: 105 Glacier (blue)
1 x 1¾oz (50g) ball—approx. 144yd (132m)—each of:
A: 108 Lime (green)
B: 115 Lipstick (bright pink)
C: 104 Powder (pale pink)
D: 103 Chick (yellow)

US size E/4 (3.5mm) crochet hook

gauge

10 rows x 3½ patterns over 4in. (10cm) square, working 5 shell stitch using US size E/4 (3.5mm) hook and Louisa Harding Cassia yarn.

finished measurement

To fit a hot water bottle 7½in. (19cm) wide x 10½in. (26cm) long (to shoulder) with a top measuring approx. 5in. (13cm)

note

The multiple is 6 sts + 1 st (+ 1 for the base ch) (see page 18).

abbreviations

approx. approximate(ly)
ch chain
dc double crochet
MC main color
rep repeat
RS right side
sc single crochet
st(s) stitch(es)
ss slip stitch
tr treble
WS wrong side

back

Using MC, make 38ch.
Row 1 (RS): 1sc in second ch from hook, *miss 2 ch, 5dc in next ch (Shell made), miss 2 ch, 1sc in next ch; rep from * to end, ending 1sc in last st.
Row 2: 1ch, 3dc in first st, *miss 2 sts, 1sc in next st (top of Shell), miss 2 sts, 5dc in next st (sc from previous Row); rep from * to end, ending with 3dc in last st.
Row 3: 1ch, 1sc in first st, *miss 2 sts, 5dc in next st, miss 2 sts, 1sc in next st; rep from * to end, ending 1sc in last st.
Rep Rows 2 and 3 until 28 rows are worked, or work measures approx. 11in. (28cm), or up to the base of the hot water bottle top, ending on a Row 2.

funnel opening:

Row 1: 1ch, ss in each of next 12 sts, 1sc in next st, miss 2 sts, 5dc in next st (sc from previous row), miss 2 sts, 1sc in next st, miss next 2 sts, 5dc in next st, miss 2 sts 1sc in next st, ss in each st to end. Fasten off. Turn.

tip

The Cozy is made in three pieces: the Back, Front Bottom and Front Top.

Row 2: Miss ss from previous row and join MC in last sc made. 1ch, 5dc in same st, miss 2 sts, 1sc in next st (top of shell), 5dc in next st (sc from previous row), miss 2 sts, 1sc in next st (top of shell), miss 2 sts, 5dc in first sc from Row 1.

Row 3: 1ch, 1sc in first st, miss 1 st, 1sc in next st, miss 2 ch, 5dc in next st (sc from previous row), miss 2 sts, 1sc in next st (top of shell), miss 2 sts, 5dc in next st (sc from previous Row), miss 2 sts, 1sc in next st, miss 1 st, 1sc in last st.

Row 4: 1ch, 1sc in first st, 5dc in next st, miss 2 sts, 1sc in next st, miss 2 sts, 5dc in next st, miss 2 sts, 1sc in next st, miss 2 sts, 5dc in next st, 1sc in last st.

Row 5: 1ch, 5dc in first st, miss 2 sts, 1sc in next st, miss 2 sts, 5dc in next st, miss 2 sts, 1sc in next st, miss 2 sts, 5dc in next st, miss 2 sts, 1sc in next st, miss 1 st, 5dc in last st.

Row 6: 1ch, 3dc in first st, miss 1 st, 1sc in next st, miss 2 sts, 5dc in next st, miss 2 sts, 1sc in next st, miss 2 sts, 5dc in next st, miss 2 sts, 1sc in next st, miss 2 sts, 5dc in next st, miss 2 sts, 1sc in next st, miss 1 st, 3dc in last st.

Row 7: 1ch, 3dc, miss 2 sts, 1sc in next st (top of Shell), miss 2 sts, 5dc in next st (sc from previous row), miss 2 sts, 1sc in next st (top of Shell), miss 2 sts, 5dc in next st, miss 2 sts, 1sc in next st, miss 2 sts, 5dc in next st, miss 2 sts, 1sc in next st, miss 2 sts, 3dc in last st. Cut yarn, do not fasten off.

Row 8: Using A, 1ch, 1sc in each st to end. Fasten off.

front bottom

Work as for Back for 16 Rows (ending on a Row 2). Cut yarn, do not fasten off. Join A.

edging:

Rows 1–4: 1ch, 1sc in first st, 1sc in each st to end. (37 sts) Fasten off.

front top

Using A, make 38ch.

edging:

Row 1: 1sc in second ch from hook, 1sc in each st to end. (37 sts) Cut yarn, do not fasten off. Join MC.

main pattern:

Row 2: 1ch, 1sc in first st, *miss 2 sts, 5dc in next st, miss 2 sts, 1sc in next st; rep from * to end, ending 1sc in last st.

Row 3: 1ch, 3dc in first st, *miss 2 sts, 1sc in next st (top of Shell), miss 2 sts, 5dc in next st (sc from previous row); rep from * to end, ending with 3dc in last st.

Rep Rows 2–3 until 11 rows of pattern have been made, or approx. 4¾in. (12cm), ending on a Row 3.

funnel opening:

Rep Rows 1–7 of Funnel Opening of Back. Fasten off.

flowers

(make 3, using B, C, and D for the flowers and C, B, and A for the centers)

Using first color, make 4ch, join with a ss in first ch to form a ring.

Round 1 (RS): 1ch, 6sc in ring, break off first color, join second color with a ss in first sc.

Round 2: Using second color, *[4ch, 1tr, 4ch, 1ss] in same st, ss in next st; rep from * five times more (6 petals), working last ss in sc at base of first 4-ch. Fasten off.

finishing

Sew in ends. With RS facing upward, place Back of cozy on a flat surface. With RS together place Front Top on top of Back, aligning funnel shape. With RS together and aligning bottom edges, place Front Bottom onto Back—top edge of Front Bottom will overlap bottom edge of Front Top.

Pin Front and Back pieces together along sides and bottom only, leaving funnel opening and overlapping sc edges open. Sew pinned seams, then turn cozy RS out.

Using A, join yarn with a ss in any two loops at back of WS of a Flower near center of Round 1.

Make between 4ch and 6ch for stalk (to make a variation on length), then with RS of cozy facing, join Flower with a ss in any two loops to center of top at base of Front Top. Fasten off and sew in ends.

Attach all Flowers in the same way.

Fit onto hot water bottle.

jelly jar tea light cozies

These are perfect over little jelly jars. They are made using a fine lace yarn and a lace stitch, so that when the candlelight glows through it creates gorgeous textured patterns.

materials

Debbie Bliss Rialto Lace, 100% extra fine merino laceweight yarn
1 x 1¾oz (50g) ball—approx. 427yd (390m)—each of:
07 Fuchsia (bright pink)
033 Candy (pink)
028 Primrose (yellow)
026 Coral (salmon)
018 Aqua (deep aqua)
035 Acid Yellow (yellow-green)

US size C/2 (2.5mm) crochet hook

gauge

26 sts x 12 rows over 4in. (10cm) square, working double crochet crochet using US size C/2 (2.5mm) hook and Debbie Bliss Rialto Lace.

finished measurement

To fit a 6.5fl oz (190ml) round jelly jar

abbreviations

approx. approximate(ly)
ch chain
CL cluster
dc double crochet
dc3tog double crochet 3 stitches together
rep repeat
RS right side
sc single crochet
sp space
st(s) stitch(es)
ss slip stitch
tch turning chain
yoh yarn over hook

special abbreviations

3dcCL 3 double crochet cluster—yoh, insert hook in sp, yoh, pull yarn through work (3 loops on hook). Yoh, pull yarn through 2 loops on hook (2 loops on hook). Yoh, insert hook in same sp, yoh, pull yarn through work (4 loops on hook). Yoh, pull yarn through 2 loops on hook (3 loops on hook). Yoh, insert hook in same sp, yoh, pull yarn through work (5 loops on hook). Yoh, pull yarn through 2 loops on hook (4 loops on hook). Yoh, pull yarn through all 4 loops on hook (1 loop on hook).

4dcCL 4-double crochet together cluster (made over 2 sps)—yoh, insert hook in sp, yoh, pull yarn through work (3 loops on hook). Yoh, pull yarn through first two loops on hook (2 loops on hook). Yoh, insert hook in same sp, yoh pull yarn through work (4 loops on hook). Yoh, pull yarn through first two loops on hook (3 loops on hook). Yoh, insert hook in next sp, yoh, pull yarn though (5 loops on hook). Yoh, pull yarn through first two loops on hook (4 loops on hook). Yoh, insert hook in same sp, yoh, pull yarn through work (6 loops on hook). Yoh, pull yarn through first two loops on hook (5 loops on hook). Yoh, pull yarn through all 5 loops on hook (1 loop on hook).

cozy

(make 1 in each color)

bottom edging:

Row 1: Make 45ch, 1sc in second ch from hook, 1sc in each ch to end. (44 sts)

Row 2: 1ch, 1sc in each st to end. (44 sts)

Row 3 (increase row): 1ch, *1sc in each of next 8 sts, 2sc in next st; rep from * to last 8 sts, 1sc in each of next 7 sts, 2sc in last st. (49 sts)

main pattern:

Row 1 (RS): 1ch, 1sc in first st, 1sc in next st, *4ch, 4dcCL over next 5 sts as follows; leaving last loop of each st on hook work 1dc into each of next 2 sts, miss 1 st, 1dc into each of next 2 sts, yoh and draw through all 5 loops on hook; 4ch, 1sc in next st **, 1ch miss 1 st, 1sc in next st; rep from * ending last rep at **, 1sc in last st.

Row 2: 3ch (counts as 1dc), 1dc in first st, *3ch, 1sc in next 4-ch sp, 1ch, miss CL, 1sc in next 4-ch sp, 3ch, miss 1sc **, 3dcCL in next 1ch sp; rep from * ending last rep at **, dc2tog in last sc.

Row 3: 1ch, 1sc in first st, *1sc in next ch sp, 4ch, 4dcCL as follows: leaving last loop of each st on hook work 2dc in same ch sp, miss [1sc, 1ch, 1sc], 2dc in next ch sp, yoh and draw through all 5 loops on hook; 4ch, 1sc in same ch sp **, 1ch, rep from * ending last rep at **, 1sc in top of 3-ch from previous row.

Rep Rows 2 and 3 three times more, then rep Row 2 once more.

top edging:

Row 1: 1ch, 3sc in first ch sp, miss 1 sc, 1sc in next 1-ch sp, miss 1 sc, [3sc in next 4-ch sp] twice, miss 1 sc, 1sc in next 1-ch sp, miss 1 sc, *3sc in next ch sp, 3sc in next ch sp, miss 1 sc, 1sc in next 1-ch sp, miss 1 sc; rep from * three times more, 3sc in last ch sp, 1sc in top of dc2tog from previous row, 1sc in top of tch. (44 sts)

Rows 2–5: 1ch, 1sc in each st. (44 sts)

Work more sc rows to top lip of jar if necessary.

Fasten off

finishing

With RS together, join seam.

Turn RS out and fit over jelly jar.

bow egg cozies

These cute little things are to place over your eggs to keep them warm, but you won't want to take them off because they're so gorgeous. They make a great gift for a celebration breakfast.

materials

Debbie Bliss Rialto 4ply, 100% merino wool fingering (4ply) weight yarn
1 x 1¾oz (50g) ball—approx. 197yd (180m) per ball—each of:
22 Fuchsia (bright pink)
45 Tangerine (orange)
34 Blush (pale pink)
37 Sea green (aqua blue/green)
39 Amber (yellow)
33 Hyacinth (blue)

US size D/3 (3mm) crochet hook

25 Size 6 seed beads in white for each cozy

gauge

Approx. 20 sts x 25 rows over 4in. (10cm) square, working single crochet using US size D/3 (3mm) hook and Debbie Bliss Rialto 4ply yarn.

finished measurement

Approx. 1⅜in. (6cm) diameter

abbreviations

approx. approximate(ly)
ch chain
cont continu(e)(ing)
rep repeat
RS right side
sc single crochet
sc2tog single crochet 2 stitches together
st(s) stitch(es)
ss slip stitch
WS wrong side
yoh yarn over hook

special abbreviation

PB place bead—*On a WS row*, insert hook in next sc, yoh, pull yarn through (2 loops now on hook), slide bead up close to work, yoh, pull yarn through both loops on hook to complete beaded sc.

tip for beaded crochet

Remember to thread all the beads on the yarn before beginning to crochet.

Note that the beaded single crochet stitches are worked on WS rows so that the beads are snugly positioned on the RS of the crochet.

colorways

Cozy 1: Blush; Bow: Fuchsia
Cozy 2: Fuchsia; Bow: Blush
Cozy 3: Tangerine; Bow: Fuchsia
Cozy 4: Amber; Bow: Hyacinth
Cozy 5: Sea Green; Bow: Amber
Cozy 6: Hyacinth; Bow: Tangerine

. . . .

cozy

Thread 24 beads onto yarn.
Make 2ch, 6sc into second ch from hook.
Round 1 (RS): 2sc in each sc to end. (12 sc)
Cont in rounds with RS always facing.
Round 2: Rep Round 1. (24 sc)
Round 3: *1sc in next st, 2sc in next st; rep from
* to end. (36 sc)
Rounds 4–9: 1sc in each sc to end.
Round 10: *1sc in next sc, sc2tog over next
2 sc; rep from * to end, join with a ss in first sc
of round. (24 sts)
Turn work.
Round 11 (WS): PB in each st to end, join with
a ss in first st. (24 beaded sts)
Fasten off.

bow

Make 12ch, join with a ss in first ch to form
a circle.
Round 1: 1sc in each ch to end. (12 sts)
Round 2: 1sc in each st to end. (12 sts)
Ss in first st and fasten off leaving a long tail.

finishing

Sew in ends on WS of Cozy and turn RS out.

On Bow, sew in first end on WS. Turn RS out.
Thread remaining bead onto long tail from
fasten-off end, then thread tail into a yarn sewing
needle. Flatten piece with fasten-off st in center at
back. Wrap tail around center to create Bow
shape, then sew to secure end, incorporating
bead threaded onto yarn in center of wrap.

Sew Bow onto top of Cozy.

Vase Cozy

A lovely easy project and a great starting point in crocheting in the round for a beginner. You don't have to count the rows as you work—just keep crocheting until you reach the required length.

materials

cozy

Debbie Bliss, Rialto DK, 100% wool light worsted (DK) weight yarn
1 x 1¾oz (50g) ball—approx. 115yd (105m)—each of:
MC: 70 Pool (blue)
61 Plum (lilac)
858 Pink (pink)

edging

Debbie Bliss Rialto DK, 100% merino wool light worsted (DK) weight yarn
1 x 1¾oz (50g) ball—approx. 115yd (105m)—of:
A: 058 Grass (green)

flowers and French knots

Louisa Harding Cassia 75% superwash wool, 25% nylon light worsted (DK) weight yarn
1 x 1¾oz (50g) ball—approx. 144yd (132m)—each of:
B: 103 Chick (yellow)
      115 Lipstick (bright pink)
      104 Powder (pale pink)

US size D/3 (3mm) crochet hook

US size G/6 (4mm) crochet hook

Stitch marker

gauge

19 sts x 20 rows over 4in. (10cm) square, working single crochet using US size G/6 (4mm) hook and Debbie Bliss Rialto DK.

finished measurement

To fit a vase approx. 4in. (10cm) diameter x 6in. (15cm) high

note

The multiple for the edging is 6 sts (see page 18).

abbreviations

approx approximate(ly)
ch chain
MC main color
rep repeat
RS right side
sc single crochet
st(s) stitch(es)
ss slip stitch
WS wrong side

cozy

(any multiple of stitches)
Foundation chain: Using US size G/6 (4mm) crochet hook and MC, make 52ch. Join Foundation chain with a ss.
Insert stitch marker.
Round 1: 1sc in same place as ss, 1sc in each ch to end. (52 sts)
Round 2: 1sc in first and each sc to end. (52 sts)
Rep Round 2 until work measures height of vase or 5¾in. (14.5cm).
Next row (decrease): *1sc in each of next 11 sts, sc2tog; rep from * to end. (48 sts)
Fasten off.

edging:

Working on WS of work and using US size G/6 (4mm) crochet hook, join A with a ss in any stitch on top edge. *5ch, ss in same st, 7ch, ss in next st, 5ch, ss in same st, 1sc in each of next 4 sts; rep from * to end. Join with a ss in first sc.

Fasten off.

flowers

(make 1 in each color)

Using US size D/3 (3mm) crochet hook and B, 4ch, join ring with a ss in first ch. 1sc in ring, 5ch, ss in same sc, *1sc in ring, 5ch, ss in same sc; rep from * four more times, ss in first sc to join.

Fasten off.

finishing

Sew in ends and turn on Cozy RS out.

Sew in ends on Flower. Make a French knot in the center of each in a contrasting color. Sew Flowers onto RS in center of the Cozy.

Fit Cozy onto vase with RS facing outward.

tip for crocheting in a circle

Make sure that the chain is not twisted when you join the foundation chain circle, and count carefully in the first round to make sure you have the correct number of stitches (52).

chunky cafetière cozy

A very basic single crochet stitch and superchunky yarn are used to make this great cafetière cozy—it's very quick to make and perfect for keeping coffee warm.

materials

Debbie Bliss Lara, 58% wool, 42% alpaca chunky yarn
1 x 3½oz (100g) ball—approx. 65yd (60m)—of:
MC: 01 Pasha (off white)

Debbie Bliss Baby Cashmerino, 55% wool/33% acrylic/12% cashmere sport weight (lightweight DK) yarn
1 x 1¾oz (50g) ball—approx. 137yd (125m)—of:
A: 92 Orange (orange)

US size L/11 (8mm) crochet hook
2 leather buttons

gauge

7 sts x 8 rows over a 4in. (10cm) square, working single crochet using size US size L/11 (8mm) hook and Debbie Bliss Lara yarn.

finished measurement

7 x 7in. (17.5 x 17.5cm), to fit a medium-size 4–6 cup cafetière approx. 12in. (30cm) circumference

note

The multiple is any number of sts (+ 1 for the base ch) (see page 18).

abbreviations

approx. approximate(ly)
ch chain
MC main color
rep repeat
RS right side
sc single crochet
st(s) stitch(es)

• •

cozy

Row 1 (RS): Using MC, make 25ch, 1sc in second ch from hook, 1sc in each ch to end. (24 sts)
Rows 2–13: 1ch, 1sc in each st to end. (24 sts)
If necessary make less or more rows to fit height of cafetière.
Do not fasten off.
Row 14 (button loop): 4ch, 1sc into each st to end.
Fasten off.

finishing

With RS together join top of side seams for approx. 1in. (2.5cm), leaving remaining seam open. Turn RS out.
Sew first button to correspond with button loop. Sew second button approx. ⅜in. (1cm) from edge on same side as first button. Use holes between stitches as buttonhole for second button.
Make 2 tassels using A, and attach next to each other to RS at top edge.

cold bottle cozy

This is a great cozy for your cold water bottle—it provides shade from the sunlight and makes it easy to spot your bottle on the shelf at the gym. The pattern uses a wave and chevron stitch in stripes.

materials

Debbie Bliss Rialto DK, 100% merino wool light worsted (DK) weight yarn
1 x 1¾oz (50g) ball—approx. 115yd (105m)—each of:
A: 069 Citrus (yellow)
B: 056 Tangerine (orange)
C: 019 Duck Egg (blue)

US size E/4 (3.5mm) crochet hook

20in. (50cm) ribbon

gauge

18 sts x 15 pattern rows over 4in. (10cm) square, working Wave and Chevron pattern stitch using US size E4 (3.5mm) hook and Debbie Bliss Rialto DK.

finished measurement

Approx. 9 x 6½in. (22.5 x 16.5cm), to fit a 18.5fl oz (550ml) water bottle

note

The multiple is 6 sts + 1 st (+ 1 for the base ch) (see page 18).

abbreviations

approx. approximate(ly)
ch chain
cont continu(e)(ing)
hdc half double crochet
rep repeat
RS right side
sc single crochet
sc2tog single crochet 2 stitches together
sc3tog single crochet 3 stitches together
sp space
ss slip stitch
st(s) stitch(es)
tr treble

· ·

cozy

Using A, make 37ch, 1sc in second ch from hook, 1sc in each ch to end. (36 sts)
Row 1 (RS): Cont with A, 1ch, miss first st, *1hdc in next st, 1dc in next st, 3tr in next st, 1dc in next st, 1hdc in next st, 1sc in next st; rep from * ending last sc in top of first ch from previous row.
Cut yarn, do not fasten off.
Row 2: Join B, 1ch, 1sc in each of next 3 sts, *3sc in next st (center of 3-tr from previous row), 1sc in each of next 2 sts, sc3tog over next 3 sts, 1sc in each of next 2 sts; rep from * to last 6 sts, 1sc in each of next 2 sts, 3sc in top of next st (center of 3-tr from previous row), 1sc in each of next 2 sts, sc2tog over last st and 1ch from previous row.
Cut yarn, do not fasten off.

Row 3: Join C, 1ch, miss first sc2tog from previous row, 1sc in each of next 3 sts, *3sc in next st, 1sc in each of next 2 sts, sc3tog over next 3 sts, 1sc in each of next 2 sts; rep from * to last 5 sts, 3sc in next st, 1sc in each of next 2 sts, sc2tog over last 2 sts.

Row 4: 4ch, miss first sc2tog from previous row, 1tr in next st, *1dc in next st, 1hdc in next st, 1sc in next st, 1hdc in next st, 1dc in next st, tr3tog over next 3 sts; rep from * ending last rep tr2tog over last 2 sts.

Row 5: 1ch, miss first st, 1sc in each st to end. (36 sts).

Cut yarn, do not fasten off.

Row 6: Join A, 1ch, miss first st, 1sc in each st to end.

Rows 7–18: Rep Rows 1–6 twice more.

Rows 19–20: Rep Rows 1–2.

Row 21: Using C, rep Row 2.

Row 22: Using A, rep Row 3.

Fasten off.

finishing

Press and then sew in ends. With RS together, join seam. Turn Cozy RS out.

Tie ribbon around center of bottle to decorate.

glass bottle cozy

These look very pretty sitting on the shelf and would make an unusual and original gift wrap for a homemade liqueur or cordial. They are made using crochet circles, which are joined as you go.

materials

Debbie Bliss Baby Cashmerino, 55% wool/33% acrylic/12% cashmere sport weight (lightweight DK) yarn
1 x 1¾oz (50g) ball—approx. 137yd (125m)—each of:
A: 78 Lipstick (bright pink)
B: 601 Baby Pink (pale pink)
C: 02 Apple (green)
D: 10 Lilac (lilac)
E: 100 White (white)
F: 66 Amber (yellow)

US size D/3 (3mm) crochet hook

gauge

Four circles joined across is 14in. (10cm), using US size D/3 (3mm) hook and Debbie Bliss Baby Cashmerino yarn.

finished measurement

Approx. 6in. (15cm) high x 7¾in. (20cm) circumference

abbreviations

approx. approximate(ly)
ch chain
dc double crochet
rep repeat
RS right side
st(s) stitch(es)
ss slip stitch
yoh yarn over hook

colorway

For Cozy 1 make each Circle in A
For Cozy 2 make the Circles in A, B, C, D, E, or F

. . . .

cozy

Working on RS throughout.
Row 1:
Circle 1: 4ch, join with a ss to form a ring, 3ch, (counts as first dc), 11dc in ring, join with a ss in top of first 3-ch. (12 sts)
Fasten off.
Circle 2: 4ch, join with a ss to form a ring, 3ch (counts as first dc), 5dc in ring, take hook out of loop, insert loop into top of any st of Circle 1, insert hook back into dropped loop, yoh, pull yarn through loop on hook and st from previous circle, make another 6dc into ring of Circle 2 (12 sts). Join with a ss in top of first 3-ch.
Fasten off.
Circle 3: 4ch, join with a ss to form a ring, 3ch (counts as first dc), join with a ss to form a ring, 3ch (counts as first dc), 5dc in ring, take hook out of loop, insert hook into top of sixth st from previous joined Circles, insert hook back into dropped loop, yoh, pull yarn through loop on hook and st from previous circle, make another 6dc in ring of Circle 3. Join with a ss in top of first 3-ch. (12 sts)
Fasten off.
Circles 4–7: Rep Circle 3.
Working on Circles from Row 1, join next row of Circles from right to left.

Row 2:
Circle 2: 4ch, join with a ss to form a ring, 3ch (counts as first dc), 4dc in ring, take hook out of loop, insert hook into fourth st back from left-hand join of two circles below, insert hook back into dropped loop, yoh, pull yarn through loop and st on hook, make another 3dc in ring, take hook out of loop, insert hook into third st from previous joined Circles (on same Row), insert hook back into dropped loop, yoh, pull yarn through loop and st on hook, make 4dc more into ring. Join with a ss in top of first 3-ch. (12 sts)
Fasten off.
Rep Circle 2 until all Circles on row have been joined.
Sew in ends at the end of each row.

Row 3: Rep Row 2 until 6 rows have been worked or to required height.
Fasten off.

finishing

With RS together, join seam by stitching the matching circles together using yarn sewing needle.

Slip Cozy onto bottle.

embroidered beaded hot water bottle cozy

This pretty and delicate hot water bottle cover is decorated with embroidery stitches and beads.

materials

Louisa Harding Cassia, 75% superwash wool/25% nylon light worsted (DK) weight yarn

1¾oz (50g) balls—approx. 144yd (132m) per ball:
2 balls of MC: 104 Powder (pale pink)
1 ball of A: 115 Lipstick (bright pink)

Scrap of Louisa Harding Cassia 108 Lime (green)

US size E/4 (3.5mm) crochet hook

Embroidery thread in variegated citrus (green)

Approx. 113 Size 6 beads in frosted white

Approx. 50 Size 8 beads, AB clear

gauge

Approx. 19 sts x 13 rows over 4in. (10cm) square working half double crochet using US size E/4 (3.5mm) hook and Louisa Harding Cassia yarn.

finished measurement

To fit a hot water bottle 7½in. (19cm) wide x 10½in. (26cm) long (to shoulder) with a funnel measuring approx. 2⅜in. (6cm).

note

The multiple is any number of sts (+ 2 for the base ch) (see page 18).

abbreviations

approx. approximate(ly)
ch chain
dc double crochet
hdc half double crochet
MC main color
rep repeat
RS right side
sc single crochet
st(s) stitch(es)
ss slip stitch
WS wrong side

back

Row 1 (RS): Using MC, make 38ch, 1hdc in third ch from hook, 1hdc in each ch to end. (36 sts)
Row 2: 2ch (does not count as hdc), 1hdc in each st to end. (36 sts)
Rep Row 2 until work measures approx. 10½in (26cm) or until it reaches base of funnel, ending on a RS Row.

funnel opening:
Row 1: ss in next 12 sts, 1sc in each of next 12 sts, ss in next 12 sts. Fasten off.
Row 2: Turn. Join yarn in first sc from Row 1, working on 12 sc made in Row 1 only, 1ch, 1sc in same st, 1sc in each st to end. (12 sts)
Row 3: 1ch, 1sc in first and each st to end. (12 sts)
Row 4: 1ch, 2sc in first st, 1sc in each st to last st, 2sc in last st. (14 sts)
Row 5: 1ch, 2sc in first st, 1sc in each st to last st, 2sc in last st. (16 sts)
Row 6: Rep Row 4. (18 sts)
Row 7: Rep Row 4. (20 sts)
Row 8: Rep Row 3. (20 sts)
Row 9: Rep Row 4. (22 sts)
Row 10: Rep Row 4. (24 sts)
Cut yarn, do not fasten off.

picot edge:
Next Row (RS): Join A, 1ch, 1sc in same st, 1sc in each of next two sts, *[3ch, ss in first ch], 1sc in each of next 2 sts; rep from * to end, 1sc in last st.
Fasten off.

tip

The Cozy is made in three pieces: the Back, Front Top, and Front Bottom.

front top

Rep as for Back until work measures approx. 5½in. (14cm).
funnel opening:
Rep as for Back Funnel Opening.

front bottom

Work as for Back until work measures approx. 5¾in. (14.5cm), finishing on a WS Row.
Cut yarn, do not fasten off.
front bottom edging:
Row 1 (WS): Join A, 1ch, 1sc in first st, 1sc in each st to end. (36 sts)
Row 2 (RS): 1ch, 1sc in first st, *miss next 2 sts, 5dc in next st, miss next 2 sts, 1sc in next st; rep from * to end.
Fasten off.
front top edging:
Work on underside of Foundation chain.
Row 1 (WS): With WS facing, join A in first ch, 1ch, 1sc in same ch, 1sc in each ch to end. (36 sts)
Row 2 (RS): 1ch, 1sc in first st, *miss next 2 sts, 5dc in next st, miss next 2 sts, 1sc in next st; rep from * to end.
Fasten off.

finishing

Sew in ends.
With RS facing upward, place Back of cozy on a flat surface. With RS together place Front Top on top of Back, aligning funnel shape. With RS together and aligning bottom edges, place Front Bottom onto Back—top edge of Front Bottom will overlap bottom edge of Front Top.
Pin Front and Back pieces together along sides and bottom only, leaving funnel opening and overlapping double shell edges open. Sew pinned seams, then turn cozy RS out.

Embroider main stems with embroidery thread. Make flower stems in straight stitch with a French knot at end, using embroidery thread—see pages 20-21 for how to work embroidery stitches. Sew clusters of beads to end of each flower stem.

bobble tea cozy

This is a great tea cozy—the pattern is a Bobble stitch worked in stripes, with an added touch of bright pink from the pompoms.

materials

Louisa Harding Cassia, 75% superwash wool/25% nylon light worsted (DK) weight yarn
1¾oz (50g) balls—approx. 144yd (132m) per ball:
2 balls of A: 112 Prince (blue)
3 balls of B: 102 Ecru (off white)
1 ball of C: 108 Lime (green)
1 ball of D: 115 Lipstick (pink)

US size G/6 (4mm) crochet hook

US size J/10 (6mm) crochet hook

gauge

Approx. 4 bobbles across (12 sts) x 3 bobble rows (11 rows) over 4in. (10cm) square, using US size G/6 (4mm) hook and Louisa Harding Cassia yarn held double.

finished measurement

To fit standard sized 5-cup tea pot

note

The multiple is 3 sts + 1 st (+ 1 for the base ch) (see page 18).

tip

To work with double strands of yarn when only one ball is required for the whole project, wind the ball of yarn into two balls and work with a strand from each small ball placed together.

abbreviations

approx. approximate(ly)
cont continue
dc double crochet
hdc half double crochet
rep repeat
RS right side
sc single crochet
ss slip stitch
sts stitch(es)
tch turning chain
WS wrong side
yoh yarn over hook

special abbreviation

3dcCL 3 double crochet cluster—yoh, insert hook in st, yoh, pull yarn through work (3 loops on hook). Yoh, pull yarn through 2 loops on hook (2 loops on hook). Yoh, insert hook in same st, yoh, pull yarn through work (4 loops on hook). Yoh, pull yarn through 2 loops on hook (3 loops on hook). Yoh, insert hook in same st, yoh, pull yarn through work (5 loops on hook). Yoh, pull yarn through 2 loops on hook (4 loops on hook). Yoh, pull yarn through all 4 loops on hook (1 loop on hook). Make 1ch to complete 3dcCL.

main piece

(make 2, Front and Back)

Working with double strands of yarn throughout.

Row 1 (RS): Using A and US size J/10 (6mm) hook, make 29ch, 1sc in second ch from hook, 1sc in each ch to end. (28 sts)

Row 2: 1sc in each st to end.

Cut yarn, but do not fasten off.

Rows 3–6 are main pattern rows.

Row 3: Join B, 1sc in first st, *3dcCL in next st, 1sc in each of next 2 sts; rep from * to end.

Row 4: 1sc in each st to end.

Cut yarn, but do not fasten off.

Rows 5–6: Join A, 1sc in each st to end.

Cut yarn, do not fasten off.

Change to US size G/6 (4mm) hook.

Rows 7–8: Join B, rep Rows 3 and 4.

Cut yarn, do not fasten off.

Rows 9–10: Join A, rep Rows 5 and 6.

Cut yarn, do not fasten off.

Rep Rows 7–10 until work measures approx. 6in. (15cm)—or to top of lid—ending on a Row 10.

Do not cut yarn or fasten off.

Use one strand of yarn from this point, changing colors as instructed.

top:

Row 1 (eyelets): Cont using US size G/6 (4mm) hook and A, *1sc in each of next 3 sts, 2ch, miss next 2 sts; rep from * to last 3 sts, 1sc in each of last 3 sts.

Row 2: *1sc in each of next 3 sts, 1sc in top loop of each of next 2 ch; rep from * to last 3 sts, 1sc in each of last 3 sts.

Cut yarn, do not fasten off.

Rows 3–10: Work as main pattern Rows 3–10 above.

Cut yarn, do not fasten off.

top edging:

Join C, 1ch, *1sc in each of next 3 sts, [3ch, 1sc in base of 3-ch] (picot); rep from * ending 1sc in last st.

Fasten off.

Drawstring

Using double strands of C, make a chain measuring approx. 18in. (45cm).

Fasten off.

finishing

Sew in ends. With RS of Front and Back together sew side seams using back stitch, leaving gaps for handle and spout. Turn cozy RS out.

Thread Drawstring through eyelets and gather together at top.

Using D, make 2 small pompoms and attach one at each end of Drawstring.

tip

Pin before sewing and try the cozy on your teapot to check you have left a large enough gap for the handle and the spout.

baby cozy

The most perfect cozy—a baby cozy with ears!
This is made in a gorgeous silk mix yarn in a silver
gray, but feel free to use any color you choose;
it's just important to make sure it's a lovely soft
yarn for the lucky baby.

materials

Fyberspates Scrumptious 4ply, 55% superwash merino, 45% silk
fingering (4ply) weight yarn
3[3:4] x 3½oz (100g) hanks—approx. 339yd (365m) per hank—of:
A: 318 Glisten (silver-gray)

Debbie Bliss Rialto 4ply, 100% merino wool fingering (4ply)
weight yarn
1[1:1] x 1¾oz (50g) ball—approx. 197yd (180m)—of:
B: 39 Amber (yellow)

US size C/2 (2.5mm) crochet hook

US size D/3 (3mm) crochet hook

gauge

33 sts and 18 rows over 4in. (10cm) square working patt using US
size D/3 (3mm) hook and Fyberspates Scrumptious 4ply.

finished measurement

	Newborn	Baby	Toddler
Width	20	24	30in.
	50	62	77cm
Length	23½	27½	33½in.
	60	70	85cm

abbreviations

approx. approximate(ly)

ch chain

cont continu(e)(ing)

dc double crochet

hdc half double crochet

patt pattern

rep repeat

RS right side

sc single crochet

st(s) stitch(es)

sp space

ss slip stitch

tch turning chain

tr treble

WS wrong side

yoh yarn over hook

special abbreviations

1hdcV-st 1 half double crochet V-stitch–[1hdc, 1ch, 1hdc] into next st or sp as directed.

hdc2tog yoh, insert hook into next st and draw through loop, rep into next st (5 loops on hook), yoh and draw loop through 5 loops (1 loop on hook).

• •

main piece

Using US size C/2 (2.5mm) hook and A, make 170[197:239]ch.

Foundation row (RS): 1hdc into third ch from hook, 1hdc in each ch to end. (169[196:238] sts)

Change to US size D/3 (3mm) hook.

Row 1 (WS): 1ch, 1hdc in each of first 2 hdc, miss 1 st, *1hdcV-st in next st, miss 2 sts; rep from * to end, working last rep as 1hdcV-st in next st, miss 1 st, 1hdc in next st, 1hdc in top of tch of previous row. (55[64:78] patt with 2 hdc at each end)

Row 2 (patt row): 1ch, 1hdc in each of first 2 hdc, miss 1 hdc and 1 ch, *1hdcV-st in next st, miss next hdc and 1-ch; rep from * to end, working last rep as 1hdcV-st in next st, 1hdc in each of last 2 sts.

Rep last row until work measures approx. 23[27:33]in. (58.5[68.5:83.5]cm), ending with RS facing for next row.

left corner shaping:

Next row: 1ch, 1hdc in each of first 2 hdc, miss 1 hdc and 1 ch, *1hdcV-st in next st, miss next hdc and 1-ch; rep from * to last 5 sts, miss 3 sts, 1hdc in each of last 2 sts. (1 patt decrease)

Next row (decrease): 2ch (counts as first hdc), 1hdc in next st, miss next hdc and ch, 1hdc in next hdc, *miss next hdc and 1ch, 1hdcV-st in next st; rep from * to end, working last rep as 1hdcV-st in next st, miss 1 st, 1hdc in next st, 1hdc in top of tch. (1 patt decrease, 53[62:76] patts)

Change to US size C/2 (2.5mm) hook.

Next row: 2ch (counts as first hdc), 1hdc in each st to last 5 sts, [hdc2tog over next 2 sts] twice, 2ch, ss in top of tch.

Fasten off.

hood

Using US size C/2 (2.5mm) hook and A, make 129[141:171]ch.

Foundation row (RS): 1hdc into third ch from hook, 1hdc in each ch to end. (128[140:170] sts)

Change to US size D/3 (3mm) hook.

Row 1 (WS): 1ch, 1hdc in first hdc, miss 1 st, *1hdcV-st in next st, miss 2 sts; rep from * to end, working last rep as 1hdcV-st in next st, miss 1 st, 1hdc in top of tch.

Next row (decrease): 2ch, miss first 2 hdc and 1 ch, 1hdc in next hdc, *miss 2 sts, 1hdcV-st in next st; rep from * to last 4 sts, miss 1 hdc and 1 ch, 1hdc in next hdc. (2 patts decrease, 40[44:54] patts)

Next row: 1ch, 1hdc in first hdc, *miss 2 sts, 1hdcV-st in next st; rep from * to end, 1hdc in top of tch.

Rep last 2 rows 5[6:7] times more. (30[32:40] patts)

Next row: Work decrease row as above.

Rep last row until 2 patt remain.

Fasten off.

ears

(make 2 in A for outer ear and 2 in B for inner ear)

Using US size C/2 (2.5mm) hook, make 12ch.

Row 1(RS): 1hdc into second ch from hook, 1hdc in each of next 9 ch, 3hdc in next ch, 1hdc into each ch on opposite side of ch, turn. (23 hdc)

Row 2 (WS): 2ch (counts as 1 st), miss first st, 1hdc in each of next 10 hdc, 3hdc in next st, 1hdc in each of next 10 hdc, 1hdc in top of tch, turn. (25 sts)

Row 3: 1ch, 1sc in each of first 3 hdc, 1hdc in each of next 3 hdc, [1dc in next hdc, 2dc in next hdc] 6 times, 1dc in next hdc, 1hdc in each of next 3 hdc, 1sc in each of next 2 hdc, 1sc in top of tch. (31 sts)

Row 4: 1ch, 1sc in each of first 2 sts, 1dc in each of next 3 sts, [2tr in next st] 21 times, 1dc in each of next 3 sts, 1sc in each of next 2 sts. (52 sts)
Fasten off.

finishing

Place WS of outer Ear to WS of inner Ear. With inner Ear facing, rejoin A to lower edge of Ear and work 1 round of sc through both layers.
Fasten off.

With RS of Hood and RS of Main Piece facing each other, position Hood to left-hand corner of Main Piece, matching shaping, and pin in place. Using US size C/2 (2.5mm) hook and A, join outer edge using one row of sc.
Fasten off.
Fold Hood back so that WS faces WS of Main Piece.
Sew Ears in place on Hood.

outer edging

Using US size D/3 (3mm) hook, rejoin A to any edge of Body, work one round of sc around edges and across rim of Hood, working 3sc into each corner.
Break yarn, join in B and work 1 round of hdc around all outer edges, working 3hdc around each corner and working hdc2tog where hood joins body.
Fasten off.

embroidered jelly jar covers

Jars are ideal for keeping crochet hooks, pencils and crochet knick knacks at hand. These are to fit jelly jars that are all the same width, but just different heights. If your jelly jar is narrower, use fewer stitches and crochet up to the required height. The embroidery is a great way to embellish the cozies using basic stitches and knots.

materials

cozies

Louisa Harding Cassia, 75% superwash wool/25% nylon lightweight (DK) weight yarn
1 x 1¾oz (50g) ball–approx. 144yd (132m)–each of:
A: 115 Lipstick (bright pink)
B: 103 Chick (yellow)
C: 105 Glacier (blue)

US size D/3 (3mm) crochet hook

Stitch marker

Embroidery needle

pink holder:
Variegated embroidery thread: citrus (green), claret (reds/purple), damson (purple)

138 Size 10 seed beads in green

yellow holder:
Variegated embroidery thread: citrus (green), claret (reds/purple)

Scraps of green yarn

blue holder:
Variegated embroidery thread: aquarius (blue), citrus (green), carnation (pink)

gauge

20 sts x 22 rows over 4in. (10cm) square, working single crochet using US size E/4 (3.5mm) hook and Louisa Harding Cassia yarn.

finished measurement

To fit a jelly jar of approx. 9in. (23cm) circumference, and made to the required height

abbreviations

approx. approximate(ly)
ch chain
rep repeat
sc single crochet
st(s) stitch(es)
ss slip stitch

• •

holder

Foundation chain: Using A, B, or C make 44ch. Join Foundation chain with a ss. Insert stitch marker.
Round 1: 1sc in each ch to end. (44 sts)
Round 2: 1sc in each st to end. (44 sts)
Rep Round 2 until work reaches top curve of jar.
Fasten off.

finishing

Sew in ends, turn RS out.

pink holder:

Using embroidery thread, stitch flower petals using bullion knots with French knots in center. Work Feather stitch for stems and borders (see page 20 for details of embroidery stitches). Sew a bead onto tip of each stem on borders. Fit onto jelly jar.

yellow holder:

Using embroidery thread and scraps of green yarn, embroider stems and French knots. Embroider flowers using damson embroidery thread, using lazy daisy stitch, buttonhole wheels, straight stitch, and feather stitch.

blue holder:

Using embroidery thread, embroider flowers in blue and pink using lazy daisy stitch, straight stitch, and French knots. Embroider leaves in green using single chain stitches.

tip

Work the embroidery stitches loosely to keep the crochet fabric stretchy enough to fit the jar but not to slip down it.

mug cozies

These make a very cute gift, and they're also great for keeping your own cup of tea or coffee nice and warm.

materials

Debbie Bliss Rialto DK, 100% merino wool light worsted (DK) weight yarn
1 x 1¾oz (50g) ball—approx. 115yd (105m) per ball—for each cozy:
69 Citrus (yellow)
71 Jade (green)

US size E/4 (3.5mm) crochet hook

1 button per cozy

gauge

17 sts x 19 rows over 4in. (10cm) square, working single crochet using US size E/4 (3.5mm) hook and Debbie Bliss Rialto DK.

finished measurement

10¼ x 3in. (26 x 7.5cm), to fit an average sized mug

note

The multiple is 14 sts + 1 st (+ 1 for the base ch) (see page 18).

abbreviations

approx. approximate(ly)
ch chain
dc double crochet
rep repeat
RS right side
sc single crochet
ss slip stitch
st(s) stitch(es)

cozy

Row 1: Make 16ch, 1sc in second ch from hook, 1sc in each ch to end. (15 sts)
Row 2 (RS): 3ch, 3dc in first st, *miss 3 sts, 1sc in each of next 7 sts, miss 3 sts, 4dc in last st.
Row 3: 1ch, 1sc in each st to end, 1sc in top of 3-ch from previous row. (15 sts)
Row 4: 1ch, 1sc in each of first 4 sts, miss 3 sts, 7dc in next st, miss 3 sts, 1sc in last 4 sts.
Row 5: 1ch, 1sc in each st to end. (15 sts)
Row 6: 3ch, 3dc in first st, miss 3 sts, 1sc in each of next 7 sts, miss 3 sts, 4dc in last st.
Rep Rows 2-6 five more times.
Rep Rows 2-5 once more.

tab:

Row 1: Ss in each of next 4 sts, 1sc in each of next 7 sts, ss in each of next 4 sts.
Fasten off.
Row 2: With RS facing, rejoin yarn in first sc from previous Row. 1ch, 1sc in same st, 1sc in each of next 6 sts, turn. (7 sts)
Row 3: 1ch, 1sc in first st, 1sc in each of next 6 sts. (7 sts)
Row 4: Rep Row 3.
Row 5 (buttonhole): 1ch, 1sc in each of next 2 sts, miss 3 ch, 1sc in last 2 sts.
Row 6: 1ch, 1sc in each of next 2 sts, 3sc in ch sp, 1sc in each of last 2 sts.
Fasten off.

finishing

Sew in ends.
Sew on button on other side of Cozy to align with buttonhole.

chunky hot water bottle cover

I couldn't resist this yarn, which is a mix of wool and soft alpaca. It's really chunky so it crochets up quickly and it's very soft, which makes it perfect for a hot water bottle cover.

materials

Debbie Bliss Lara, 58% wool, 42% alpaca chunky yarn 2 x 3½oz (100g) balls—approx. 130yd (120m)—of: 01 Pasha (off white)

US size L/11 (8mm) crochet hook

Small amount of yarn in each of yellow, purple, pale green for pompoms

gauge

8 rows x 7 sts over a 4in. (10cm) square, working single crochet using size US size L/11 (8mm) hook and Debbie Bliss Lara yarn.

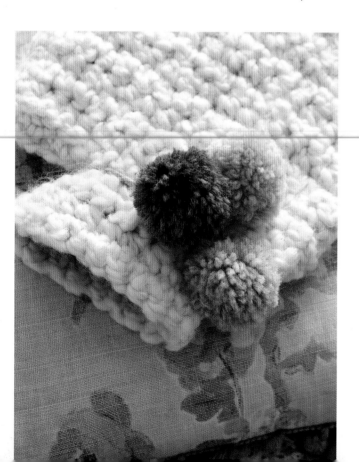

finished measurement

8½ x 12in. (21 x 30cm), to fit a hot water bottle 7½in. (19cm) wide x 10½in. (26cm) long (to shoulder) with a top funnel measuring approx. 2⅜in. (6cm)

note

The Cozy is made in three pieces: Back, Front Top, and Front Bottom. The multiple is any number of sts (+ 1 for the base ch) (see page 18).

abbreviations

approx. approximate(ly)
ch chain
rep repeat
RS right side
sc single crochet
ss slip stitch
st(s) stitch(es)

back

Row 1 (RS): Make 17ch, 1sc in second ch from hook, 1sc in each ch to end. (16 sts)
Row 2: 1ch, 1sc in each st to end. (16 sts)
Rep Row 2 until 21 rows have been made, or work measures to the top of the hot water bottle (before the funnel). Do not fasten off.
funnel opening:
Row 1: 1ch, ss in each of next 6 sts, 1sc in each of next 4 sts, ss in each of next 6 sts. Fasten off. Turn.

tip

Use a yarn sewing needle with a large eye for sewing up this project as the yarn is very chunky.

Use large plastic headed pins for pinning seams together, or use quilting pins.

Row 2: Miss slip stitches from previous row and join yarn in last sc made. 1ch, 2sc in same st, 1sc in each of next 2 sts, 2sc in last st. (6 sts)

Row 3: 1ch, 2sc in first st, 1sc in each of next 4 sts, 2sc in last st. (8 sts)

Row 4: 1ch, 2sc in first st, 1sc in each of next 6 sts, 2sc in last st. (10 sts)

Row 5: 1ch, 1sc in each st to end. (10 sts).
Fasten off.

front top

Rep Rows 1 and 2 of Back until 13 rows have been made or work measures approx. 6¼in. (16cm). Do not fasten off.
funnel opening:
Rep Top Funnel Opening as for Back.

front bottom

Rep Rows 1 and 2 of Back until 16 rows have been made, or work measures approx. 7¾in. (19.5cm).
Fasten off.

finishing

Sew in ends.
With RS facing upward, place Back of cozy on a flat surface. With RS together place Front Top on top of Back, aligning funnel shape. With RS together and aligning bottom edges, place Front Bottom onto Back—top edge of Front Bottom will overlap bottom edge of Front Top.
Pin Front and Back pieces together along sides and bottom only, leaving funnel opening and overlapping edges on front open. Sew pinned seams, then turn cozy RS out.

pompoms

Make 3 small pompoms, one in each color.
Using yellow, make a chain of approx. 7in. (17.5cm). Leaving a long end, take hook out of chain, wrap chain around neck of Cozy and lengthen loop. Thread the chain through the loop, then tighten loop. Put hook back into loop (join). Make approx. 6ch, then attach pompom by inserting hook through wrap of pompom. Fasten off.
Rejoin yarn to chain to join, make 6ch, join next pompom through wrap, as for first pompom.
Insert hook into first chain (end of remaining loop), insert hook into wrap of last pompom and attach in the same way as before.
Sew in ends.

bobble cafetière cozy

The bobble stitch used for this cozy creates a lovely thick fabric, which will keep your coffee piping hot.

materials

Debbie Bliss Blue Faced Leicester DK, 100% wool light worsted (DK) weight yarn

1 x 1¾oz (50g) ball—approx. 118yd (108m)—each of:

A: 08 Rose (pale pink)
B: 15 Sage (dark green)
C: 17 Amber (yellow)
D: 13 Pale Blue (blue)
E: 09 Fuchsia (dark pink)
F: 16 Willow (pale green)
G: 11 Heather (purple)

US size G/6 (4mm) crochet hook

1 large wooden button

2 small wooden buttons

gauge

Approx. 4 bobbles across x 10 bobble rows over 4in. (10cm) square, using US size G/6 (4mm) hook and Debbie Bliss Blue Faced Leicester DK yarn.

finished measurement

Approx. 12 x 7in. (30 x 17.5cm), to fit a medium-size 4-6 cup cafetière, approx. 12in. (30cm) circumference

note

The multiple is 4 sts + 3 sts (+ 1 for the base ch) (see page 18).

abbreviations

approx. approximate(ly)
ch chain
cont continu(e)(ing)
dc double crochet
rep repeat
RS right side
sc single crochet
sc2tog single crochet 2 stitches together
st(s) stitch(es)
ss slip stitch
WS wrong side

special abbreviation

5dcCL 5 double crochet cluster/bobble—yoh, insert hook in st, yoh, pull yarn through work (3 loops on hook). Yoh, pull yarn through first 2 loops on hook (2 loops on hook). Yoh, insert hook in same st, yoh, pull yarn through work (4 loops on hook), yoh, pull yarn through first 2 loops on hook (3 loops left on hook). Yoh, insert hook in same st, yoh, pull yarn through work (5 loops on hook), yoh, pull yarn through first 2 loops on hook (4 loops left on hook). Yoh, insert hook in same st, yoh, pull yarn through work (6 loops on hook), yoh, pull yarn through first 2 loops on hook (5 loops left on hook). Yoh, insert hook in same st, yoh, pull yarn through work (7 loops on hook), yoh, pull yarn through first 2 loops on hook (6 loops left on hook). Yoh, pull yarn through all 6 loops on hook (1 loop left on hook). Make 1ch to complete 5dcCL.

cozy

Work from top to bottom of Cozy.

Using A, make 44ch.

Row 1 (RS): 1sc in second ch from hook, 1sc in each ch to end. (43 sts)

begin bobble pattern:

Row 2 (WS): 1ch, *1sc in each of next 3 sts, 5dcCL in next st; rep from * to last 3 sts, 1sc in each of last 3 sts. (10 bobbles).
Cut yarn, do not fasten off.

Row 3: Join B, 1ch, *1sc in each of next 3 sts, 1sc in top of next 5dcCL; rep from * to last 3 sts, 1sc in each of last 3 sts.

Row 4: 1ch, 1sc in first st, 5dcCL in next st, *1sc in each of next 3 sts, 5dcCL in next st; rep from * to last st, 1sc in last st. (11 bobbles)
Cut yarn, do not fasten off.

Row 5: Join C, 1ch, 1sc in first st, *1sc in top of next 5dcCL, 1sc in each of next 3 sts; rep from * to last 5dcCL, 1sc in top of last 5dcCL, 1sc in last st.

Rep Rows 2–5, using A, B, C, D, E, F, and G to change color every two Rows until 16 bobble rows have been worked ending on a Row 5.
Fasten off.

edging:

With RS facing, join A in top left-hand corner (of Row 1).

Row 1:

Side 1

1ch, [1sc in each of next 5 rows down first side edge, sc2tog over next 2 rows] 4 times, 1sc in each row to corner (second corner), [1sc, 1ch, 1sc] in corner st.

Bottom edge

*1sc in top of 5dcCL, 1sc in each of next 3 sts; rep from * to next corner. [1sc, 1ch, 1sc] in corner st.

Side 2

[1sc in each of next 5 rows down first side edge, sc2tog over next 2 rows] 4 times, 1sc in each row to corner (third corner), [1sc, 1ch, 1sc] in corner st.

Top edge

*1sc in each of next 3 sts, 1sc in top of 5dcCL; rep from * to next corner, [1sc, 1ch, 1sc] in corner st, join with a ss in first sc.

Row 2: 1ch, work a sc edge by working 1sc in each st and 3sc in each corner ch sp, join with a ss in first sc.
Fasten off.

tab

Using A, make 13ch.

Row 1: 1sc in 8th ch from hook, 1sc in each of next 5 ch.

Row 2: 1ch, 1sc in each of next 6 sc, 1sc in each of next 3 ch, 2sc in next ch, 1sc in each of next 9 ch (working on underside of these 9 ch).

Row 3: 1ch, 1sc in each of next 9 sc, 2sc in next 2 sc, 1sc in each of next 8 sc, ss in last sc.
Fasten off.

finishing

With RS together join top of side seams for approx. 1in. (2.5cm) leaving remaining seam open.

Turn RS out.

With RS together, sew Tab to bottom of side edge, approx. ⅜in. (1cm) from corner.

Sew large button on bottom of Cozy to correspond with buttonhole on Tab.

Sew small buttons on edging: Button 1 between second and third bobble from bottom and Button 2 between second and third bobble from top, on same side as large button.

small button loops

With RS facing, and using A, join yarn to align with side of Button 1, in sc of edging on same side as Tab. 1ch, 1sc in same st, 3ch, miss 1 st, 1sc in next st. Fasten off.

Repeat for Button 2. Fasten off.

Sew in ends.

tip

When working a single crochet into the top of the 5-double crochet cluster, make the single crochet stitch into the chain at the top of the cluster.

daisy tea cozy

A very pretty summertime tea cozy for sipping tea in the garden. The cozy is made in a worsted weight using the yarn doubled, and the flowers are made using a delicate fingering yarn.

materials

main cozy

Debbie Bliss Blue Faced Leicester Aran, 100% wool worsted (Aran) weight yarn

2 x 1¾oz (50g) balls—approx. 164yd (150m)—of:

MC: 15 Mint (light green)

daisies

Debbie Bliss Rialto 4ply, 100% merino wool fingering (4ply) weight yarn

1 x 1¾oz (50g) ball—approx. 197yd (180m)—each of:

A: 39 Amber (yellow)

B: 01 White (white)

US size J/10 (6mm) crochet hook

US size D/3 (3mm) crochet hook

gauge

11 sts x 13 rows over a 4in. (10cm) square working single crochet, using US size J/10 (6mm) hook and Debbie Bliss Blue Faced Leicester Aran yarn doubled (2 strands).

finished measurement

To fit a medium-size 2-pint teapot (4–6 cups).

Approx. 7in. (17.5cm) from top to bottom, 8in. (20cm) wide from center of handle to edge of spout

abbreviations

approx. approximate(ly)

ch chain

cont continu(e)(ing)

MC main color

rep repeat

RS right side

sc single crochet

sc2tog single crochet 2 stitches together

ss slip stitch

st(s) stitch(es)

WS wrong side

yoh yarn over hook

note

Use MC yarn doubled throughout by winding main ball into two smaller balls and using 2 strands together.

main piece

(make 2, Front and Back)
Using MC double and US size J/10 (6mm) hook, make 27ch.
Row 1 (RS): 1sc in second ch from hook, 1sc in each ch to end. (26 sts)
Rows 2-4: 1ch, 1sc in each st to end. (26 sts)
Row 5: 1ch, sc2tog, 1sc in each st to last 2 sts, sc2tog. (24 sts)
Rep Row 2 until work measures 4in. (10cm). (24 sts)
Next row: 1ch, sc2tog, 1sc in each st to last 2 sts, sc2tog. (22 sts)
Rep the last row until 8 sts remain.
Next row: 1ch, [sc2tog] 4 times. (4 sts)
Next row: 1ch, 1sc in each st to end. (4 sts)
Fasten off.

tab

Using MC double and US size J/10 (6mm) hook, make 4ch.
Row 1: 1sc in second ch from hook, 1sc in each ch to end. (3 sts)
Row 2: 1ch, 1sc in each st to end. (3 sts)
Rep Row 2 thirteen times more.
Fasten off.

daisies

(make approx. 75)
Using A and US size D/3 (3mm) hook, make 4ch, ss in first ch to make a ring.
Round 1: 1ch, 9sc in ring, join with a ss in first sc.
Cut yarn but do not fasten off.
Round 2: Join B, 7ch, ss in same sc (first petal), *ss in next sc, 7ch, ss in same sc; rep from * to end. (9 petals)
Fasten off.
Sew in ends of yellow, leave one strand from white for sewing onto cozy.

finishing

With RS together, pin Front and Back of cozy with long plastic-headed pins, then slip it over your tea pot and take the pins out where the handle and spout go. I use contrasting colored yarn as stitch markers to mark these spaces. Remove the cozy from the tea pot.

Take the pin out of the top of the cozy. Fold the Tab in half. Put folded end into the top of the tea cozy and insert all the way down leaving the 2 unfolded edges in line with the top edge of the tea cozy, so you can just see them poking through. Pin this in place.

Sew up sides and top of Cozy, incorporating the Tab at the top and leaving the gaps open between the stitch markers for the handle and spout. Sew in ends, turn RS out. You'll see that the Tab is now in place with the loop sticking out at the top.

Sew Daisies onto both sides of Cozy and 1 on each side of Tab.

chapter three

cozy & tidy

passport holder

Easy to find in your purse, protects your passport and totally individual! This is a lovely V-stitch pattern and ideal as a beginner's project.

materials

Louisa Harding Cassia 75% superwash wool, 25% nylon light worsted (DK) weight yarn
1 x 1¾oz (50g) ball—approx. 144yd (132m)—each of:
A: 112 Prince (blue)
B: 101 White (white)

US size D/3 (3mm) crochet hook

Approx. 10in. (25cm) square of lining fabric

½yd (½m) of red ribbon

gauge

Approx. 9 hdcV-sts sts x 15 pattern rows over 4in. (10cm) square, using US size D/3 (3mm) hook and Louisa Harding Cassia yarn.

finished measurement

Approx. 6 x 4½in. (15 x 11.5cm)

abbreviations

approx. approximate(ly)
ch chain
hdc half double crochet
rep repeat
sc single crochet
st(s) stitch(es)
ss slip stitch
tch turning chain
WS wrong side

special abbreviations

1hdcV-st 1 half double crochet V-stitch—[1hdc, 1ch, 1hdc] into next st or sp as directed.

1scV-st 1 single crochet V-stitch—[1sc, 1ch, 1sc] into next st or sp as directed.

main piece

(make 2, Front and Back)
Work in multiples of 2 + 1.
Using A, make 21ch. 1sc in second ch from hook, 1sc in each ch to end. (20 sts)
Row 1(RS): Using A, 2ch (tch), *miss next st, 1hdcV-st in next st; rep from * to last 2 sts, miss next st, 1hdc in last st.
Row 2: Using A, 2ch (tch), *1hdcV-st in next ch sp (between previous V-sts); rep from * to end, 1hdc in top of tch. Break yarn, do not fasten off.
Row 3: Using B, 1ch (tch), *1scV-st in next ch sp (between previous V-sts); rep from * to end, 1sc in 2-ch. Break yarn, do not fasten off.
Rows 4–6: Using A, 2ch (tch), *1hdcV-st in next ch sp (between previous V-sts); rep from * to end, 1hdc in top of tch.
After Row 6, break yarn, do not fasten off.
Row 7: Rep Row 3.
Rep Rows 4–7 until work measures approx. 6in. (15cm).
Fasten off.

finishing

Block piece if necessary and sew in ends.
With RS together, join side and bottom seams.

Make and insert lining and ribbon for ties at top edge, following instructions on page 22, Method 1.

paperback cozy

Protect your books with this pretty book cozy. It makes a great gift for a bookworm, protects paperbacks and is made using a simple single crochet stitch in stripes.

materials

Debbie Bliss Blue Faced Leicester DK, 100% wool light worsted (DK) weight yarn
1 x 1¾oz (50g) ball—approx. 118yd (108m)—each of:
A: 08 Rose (pink)
B: 17 Amber (yellow)
C: 09 Fuchsia (bright pink)
D: 11 Heather (purple)
E: 16 Willow (green)
F: 13 Pale blue (blue)

US size E/4 (3.5mm) crochet hook

gauge

19 sts x 21 rows over 4in. (10cm) square, working single crochet using US size E/4 (3.5mm) hook and Debbie Bliss Blue Faced Leicester DK yarn.

finished measurement

Approx. 5½ x 8¼in. (14 x 20.5cm)

note

The multiple is any number of sts (+ 1 for the base ch) (see page 18).

abbreviations

approx. approximate(ly)
ch chain
cont continu(e)(ing)
RS right side
sc single crochet
st(s) stitch(es)
WS wrong side

. . . .

main piece

Row 1 (RS): Using A, make 26ch, 1sc in second ch from hook, 1sc in each ch to end. (25 sts)
Rows 2–5: Cont with same color, 1sc in each st to end. (25 sts) Break yarn, do not fasten off.
Each following row: Make 1ch, 1sc in each st to end, breaking yarn when color change is necessary and not fastening off.
Use colors as follows:
Two rows B.
One row C.
Two rows B.
Six rows D.
Two rows E.
One row C.
Two rows E.
Six rows F.
Two rows A.
One row C.
Two rows A.
Twenty rows E.
Two rows A.
One row C.
Two rows A.
Six rows F.
Two rows E.
One row C.
Two rows E.

Six rows D.

Two rows B.

One row C.

Two rows B.

Row 80-85: A

Fasten off.

top edging:

Join D on RS in first st of one short end.

Row 1: 1ch, 1sc in first st, 1sc in each st to end. (25 sts)

Row 2-3: 1ch, 1sc in each st to end.

Fasten off.

Repeat edging on other short end.

spines

(make 2)

These Spines are made to fit a book cover 7¾ x 5 x ¾in.

(19.5 x 13 x 2cm). They should be approx. the same length as

the Main Piece when it has been folded in half, allowing approx.

6 rows at the bottom for the width of the book.

Row 1: Using F, make 38ch, 1sc in second ch from hook, 1sc in each ch to end. (37 sts)

Rows 2-5: 1ch, 1sc in each st to end.

Fasten off.

Pin and block.

finishing

Sew in ends. Pin and block.

Fold Main Piece with WS together (RS facing). Place marker at center fold at bottom on side edge. Place marker in center of one short edge of Spine. Pin Spine lengthways down one Main Piece side edge only, with WS together and matching markers at bottom. (Remove these markers once side is pinned). Place a marker in each of two corners at bottom of Spine.

Starting at top edge, join B (yellow) with a ss through both pieces. Make a sc seam along first edge by making 34sc evenly down edge to first marker (first corner of Spine), make 2sc in corner, 2sc in along second short edge.

Take out pins along first edge just joined. Pin Spine and Main Piece along second edge. Make 34sc evenly along second edge.

Fasten off.

Repeat on other side.

crochet hook cozy

At home I keep my crochet hooks in jelly jars (see page 82 for cozy), but when I go out I like to take a portable crochet hook cozy and this is just the perfect size. It's made in the round, using spirals, and it makes a great gift for someone, with a set of crochet hooks inside.

materials

Louisa Harding Cassia, 75% superwash wool/25% nylon light worsted (DK) weight yarn

1 x 1¾oz (50g) ball—approx. 144yd (132m)—each of:

A: 112 Prince (blue)
B: 102 Ecru (off white)

US size D/3 (3mm) crochet hook

Stitch marker

1 small button

gauge

20 sts x 22 rows over 4in. (10cm) square, working single crochet using US size D/3 (3mm) hook and Louisa Harding Cassia yarn.

finished measurement

Approx. 2¼ x 8in. (5.5 x 20cm)

abbreviations

approx. approximately
ch chain
cont continu(e)(ing)
MC main color
sc single crochet
sc2tog single crochet 2 stitches together
st(s) stitch(es)
ss slip stitch

cozy

Using A, make 2ch, 6sc in second ch from hook. Place a stitch marker in loop on hook.

Round 1: 2sc in each st to end. (12 sts)
Round 2: 2sc in each st to end. (24 sts)
Rounds 3–4: 1sc in back loop of each st to end. (24 sts)

Work should now look like a small bowl curving inward. Turn work out so that ridges formed by working in back loops are on outside. Cont to work on this side of work.

Round 5: Working in both loops of each st, 1sc in each st to end. (24 sts)

Cont working 1sc in each st, in a spiral, until work measures approx. 6¾in. (17cm) or until piece is same size as length of crochet hooks.

Turn, then begin working in rows.

Next 12 rows: 1ch, 1sc in each of next 13 sts. (13 sts)
Next row: 1ch, sc2tog, 1sc in each of next 9 sts, sc2tog. (11 sts)
Next row: 1ch, 1sc in each st to end. (11 sts)
Next row: 1ch, sc2tog, 1sc in each of next 7 sts, sc2tog. (9 sts)
Next row: 1ch, 1sc in each st to end. (9 sts)
Next row: 1ch, sc2tog, 1sc in each of next 5 sts, sc2tog. (7 sts)
Next row (buttonhole): 1ch, sc2tog, 2ch, miss next 3 sts, sc2tog.
Next row: 1ch, 2sc in ch sp, ss in last st. (4 sts).

Cut yarn, do not fasten off.

edging:

Join B, 1ch, make approx. 21sc down first side, 1sc in each st along front edge, make approx. 25sc along second side and top to join. Join with a ss in first sc.

Fasten off.

finishing

Sew in ends, then sew on button to match buttonhole.

soap cozies

I travel a lot and I like to take my favorite soap with me. A soap cozy is exactly what I need to wrap it in—and I can use the cozy as a bathroom cloth afterward, dry it, then stick the soap back in it again for traveling home.

materials

For each cozy
DMC Natura Just Cotton, 100% cotton fingering (4ply) yarn
1 x 1¾oz (50g) ball—approx. 169yd (155m) per ball—for each cozy:
A: N30 Glicine (lilac)
B: N06 Rose Layette (pale pink)
C: N87 Glacier (pale blue)
D: N52 Geranium (dark pink)

US size D/3 (3mm) crochet hook

1 small button for each cozy

gauge

4 Shells across x 12 rows of Shell stitch over 4in. (10cm) square, using US size D/3 (3mm) hook and DMC Natura Just Cotton.

finished measurement

6in. (15cm) square, to fit a soap bar measuring approx. 2¾in. (7cm) square

note

The multiple is 6 sts + 1 sts (+ 1 for the base ch) (see page 18).

abbreviations

approx. approximate(ly)
ch chain
ch sp chain space
dc double crochet
rep repeat
RS right side
sc single crochet
st(s) stitch(es)
sp space
ss slip stitch
tch turning chain
WS wrong side

special abbreviation

Shell stitch—[2dc, 1ch, 2dc] in same ch or sp.

• •

cozy

Make 38ch.
Row 1 (RS): 1sc in second ch from hook. *miss next 2 ch, Shell in next ch, miss next 2 ch, 1sc in next ch; rep from * to end.
Row 2 (WS): 3ch, 2dc first sc, 1sc in 1-ch sp of next Shell; *Shell in next sc, 1sc in 1-ch sp of next Shell; rep from * to end, ending last rep with 3dc in last sc.
Row 3: 1ch, 1sc in first dc, *Shell in next sc, 1sc in 1-ch sp of next Shell; rep from * to end, working last sc of last rep in top of tch.
Rep Rows 2 and 3 until work measures 6in. (15cm) or Cozy is a square.
Do not fasten off.
button loop:
Make 6ch, join with a ss in same st.
Fasten off.

finishing

Sew in ends.
Place soap diagonally in center of WS of cozy, with button loop at top. Fold side corners over soap, fold bottom corner over top of sides, fold top corner (with button loop) down. Mark where button matches button loop and sew on button in marked place.

sunglasses case

I'm constantly leaving my sunglasses around and getting them scratched. This cozy will protect your shades and is a really fun project to make over the summer.

materials

Louisa Harding Cassia, 75% superwash wool/25% nylon light worsted (DK) weight yarn

1 x 1¾oz (50g) ball—approx. 144yd (132m)—each of:

A: 124 (dark pink)
B: 105 Glacier (pale blue)
C: 104 Powder (pale pink)
D: 107 Lilac (lilac)
E: 112 Prince (mid blue)

US size D/3 (3mm) crochet hook

Approx. 22 x 5¼in. (56 x 13cm) of cotton lining fabric

gauge

2¾in. (7cm) square using US size D/3 (3mm) hook and Louisa Harding Cassia yarn.

finished measurement

Approx. 10 x 4in. (25 x 10cm)

abbreviations

approx. approximate(ly)
ch chain
ch sp chain space
dc double crochet
rep repeat
RS right side
sc single crochet
ss slip stitch
st(s) stitch(es)

special abbreviation

2dcCL 2 double crochet cluster—yoh, insert hook in st or sp, yoh, pull yarn through work (3 loops on hook). Yoh, pull yarn through 2 loops on hook (2 loops on hook). Yoh, insert hook in same st or sp, yoh, pull yarn through work (4 loops on hook). Yoh, pull yarn through 2 loops on hook (3 loops on hook). Yoh, pull yarn through all 3 loops on hook (1 loop on hook).

colorway

Use either A, B, C, D for Rounds 1, 2, 3 and always use E for Round 4.

squares

(make 9)
Using A, make 6ch, join with a ss in first ch to form a ring.
Round 1 (RS): 4ch, [1dc, 1ch in ring] 11 times, join with a ss in third of first 4-ch.
Cut yarn, do not fasten off.
Round 2: Join B in next 1-ch sp, 3ch, 1dc in same ch sp, [3ch, 2dcCL in next ch sp] 11 times, 3ch, join with a ss in top of first 3-ch. (12 x 2dcCL)
Cut yarn, do not fasten off.
Round 3: Join C in top of next 2dcCL, 1ch, 1sc in same st, 1ch, miss first 3-ch sp and 2dcCL, *[3dc, 3ch, 3dc in next ch sp] (corner), 1ch, miss next 2dcCL and next 3-ch sp, 1sc in top of next 2dcCL, 1ch, miss next 3-ch sp and next 2dcCL; rep from * three times more, ending last rep with a ss in top of first sc.
Cut yarn, do not fasten off.
Round 4: Join D in same sc, 1ch, 1sc in same st, 1sc in first ch sp, *1sc in each of next 3 sts, 3sc in corner ch sp, 1sc in each of next 3 sts, 1sc in next ch sp, 1sc in next sc, 1sc in next ch sp; rep from * three times more, 1sc in each of next 3 sts, 3sc in corner ch sp, 1sc in each of next 3 sts, 1sc in next ch sp, join with a ss in first sc.
Fasten off.

finishing

Block and press Squares lightly.
Place Squares on a flat surface and arrange following the diagram (see opposite). Sew Squares together into the shaped piece.

Sew lining (see page 22, Method 2).

Fold piece into glasses cozy shape along dotted lines, matching letters. Pin and sew with RS together. Turn RS out.
Block and press again.

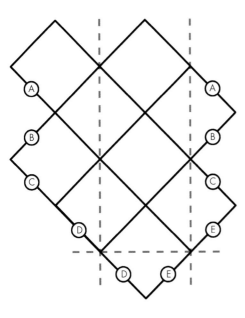

eye glasses cozy

I love the soft feel of this cozy, which is made using a delicious blend of hand-dyed silk and merino. This case is big enough to hold an average-sized pair of eye glasses.

materials

Fyberspates Scrumptious 4ply, 55% superwash merino wool, 45% silk fingering (4ply) yarn

1 x 3½oz (100g) hank—approx. 399yd (365m)—of 318 Glisten (silver-gray)

US size D/3 (3mm) crochet hook

5 Size 6 white seed beads

Small snap fastener

12 x 8in. (30 x 20cm) of cotton lining fabric

gauge

4 Shells x 13 Shell st rows over a 4in. (10cm) square using a US size D/3 (3mm) hook and Fyberspates Scrumptious 4ply yarn.

finished measurement

Approx. 5¾in. (14.5cm) wide x 3½in. (8.5cm) long (when folded with flap down)

note

The multiple is 6 sts + 1 sts (+ 1 for the base ch) (see page 18).

abbreviations

approx. approximate(ly)
ch chain
dc double crochet
dc2tog double crochet 2 stitches together
hdc half double crochet
rep repeat
RS right side
sc single crochet
sc2tog single crochet 2 stitches together
ss slip stitch
st(s) stitch(es)
WS wrong side

special abbreviations

5dc-Shell—make 5dc in same stitch.

3dc-Shell—make 3dc in same stitch.

• •

cozy

Make 38ch.
Row 1 (RS): 1sc in second ch from hook, 1sc in each ch to end. (37 sts)
Row 2: 1ch, 1sc in first st, *miss next 2 sts, 5dc in next st (5dc-Shell), miss next 2 sts, 1sc in next st; rep from * to end of row.
Row 3: 3ch, 2dc in first st, *miss next 2 sts, 1sc in next st (center st of Shell), miss next 2 sts, 5dc in next sc; rep from * to end, ending last rep with 3dc in last sc.
Row 4: 1ch, 1sc in first st, *miss next 2 sts, 5dc in next sc (5dc-Shell), miss next 2 sts, 1sc in next st (center st of Shell); rep from * ending last rep with 1sc in top of first 3-ch from previous row.
Row 5: Rep Row 3.
Rep Rows 4–5 until work measures approx. 7¼in. (18cm) ending on a Row 4.
flap:
Row 1: 3ch, 2dc in first sc, *miss next 2 sts, 1sc in next st, miss next 2 sts, 5dc in next sc; rep from * ending 3dc in last sc. (5 x 5dc-Shells)
Row 2: 1ch, miss first st, 1sc in next st (center st of 3dc-Shell), miss 1 st, 3dc in next sc, *miss 2 sts, 1sc in next st, miss 2 sts, 5dc in next sc; rep from * to end, ending 3dc in last sc, miss 2 sts, 1sc in top of 3-ch from previous row. (5 x 5dc-Shells)

Row 3: 2ch, miss first 2 sts, 1sc in next st (center of 3dc-Shell), miss next st, 3dc in next st, *miss 2 sts, 1sc in next st, miss next 2 sts, 5dc in next st; rep from * twice more, miss 2 sts, 1sc in next st, miss 2 sts, 3dc in next sc, miss next st, 1sc in next st (center of 3dc-Shell), miss next st, 1hdc in last sc. (3x 5dc-Shells)

Row 4: 2ch, miss first 3 sts, 1sc in next st, miss next st, 3dc in next st, miss next 2 sts, 1sc in next st, *miss next 2 sts, 5dc in next st, miss next 2 sts, 1sc in next st; rep from * once more, miss 2 sts, 3dc in next sc, miss next st, 1sc in next st (center of 3dc-Shell), miss next st, 1hdc in last sc. (2 x 5dc-Shells)

Row 5: 2ch, miss first 3 sts, 1sc in next st (center of 3dc-Shell), miss next st, 5dc in next st, *miss next 2 sts, 1sc in next st, miss next 2 sts, 5dc in next st; rep from * once more, miss next st, 1sc in next st (center of 3dc-Shell), miss next 2 sts, 1hdc in top of first 2-ch from previous row. (3 x 5dc-Shells)

Row 6: 3ch, miss first 4 sts, 1sc in next st, *miss next 2 sts, 5dc in next st, miss next 2 sts, 1sc in next st; rep from * once more, miss next 3 sts, 1dc in top of first 2-ch from previous row. (2 x 5dc-Shells)
Fasten off.

flower

Make 4ch, join with a ss to form a ring.
Round 1: [3ch, dc2tog in ring, 3ch, ss in ring] five times. (5 petals)
Fasten off.
Using a yarn sewing needle weave around center hole to close.
Sew 5 beads into center of flower.

finishing

Line crochet piece on WS (before sewing seams)—see page 22, Method 2 for lining instructions. With RS of crocheted piece together, fold bottom edge up to 8th row from top of Flap. With RS together, sew side seams of crochet piece. Turn RS out.

Attach snap fastener to WS at end Flap and corresponding place on main piece. Sew crochet flower on RS end of Flap (above snap fastener).

patchwork sewing machine cozy

This is a much nicer cover for your sewing machine than the plastic ones that come with the machine. Customize your own sewing machine by making this Cozy with crochet squares joined together with a single crochet seam. This doesn't need lining, but a lining will prevent the cotton reel holder from poking through the holes of the crochet stitches.

materials

Debbie Bliss Baby Cashmerino, 55% wool/33% acrylic/12% cashmere sport weight (lightweight DK) yarn
2 x 1¾oz (50g) balls—approx. 274yd (250m)—of:
A: 101 (off white)
1 x 1¾oz (50g) ball—approx. 137yd (125m)—each of:
B: 68 Peach Melba (peach)
C: 18 Citrus (green)
D: 83 Butter (yellow)
E: 59 Mallard (teal blue)
F: 202 Light Blue (pale blue)

US size G/6 (4mm) crochet hook

½yd (½m) of cotton fabric

gauge

Each square measures approx. 4in. (10cm), using US size G/6 (4mm) hook and Debbie Bliss Baby Cashmerino yarn.

finished measurement

To fit a standard-sized sewing machine, 16 x 12 x 4in. (40 x 30 x 10cm)

abbreviations

approx. approximately
ch chain
ch sp chain space
dc double crochet
hdc half double crochet
rep repeat
RS right side
sc single crochet
ss slip stitch
sp(s) space(s)
st(s) stitch(es)
WS wrong side

colorway

Make a total of 34 squares in the following colors:
Off white x 5
Peach x 6
Green x 5
Yellow x 6
Teal blue x 5
Pale blue x 7

· ·

squares

Using one color per square (A, B, C, D, E, or F). Make 6ch, join with a ss to form a ring.
Round 1 (RS): 3ch (counts as 1dc), 15dc in ring, join with a ss in top of first 3-ch. (16 sts)
Round 2: 4ch (counts as 1dc, 1ch), [1dc, 1ch] in next st 15 times, join with a ss in third of first 4-ch. (16 dc)
Round 3: 3ch, *1dc in next ch sp, 1dc in next st; rep from * to end, ending 1dc in last ch sp, join with a ss in top of first 3-ch. (32 dc)

Round 4: 3ch (counts as 1dc), [4dc, 3ch, 5dc] in same place as ss (corner), miss 2 sts, 1sc in next st, 5dc in next st, 1sc in next st, miss 2 sts, *[5dc, 3ch, 5dc] in next st (corner), miss 2 sts, 1sc in next st, 5dc in next st, 1sc in next st, miss 2 sts; rep from * to end, join with a ss in top of first 3-ch.

Round 5: 4ch, miss first 5 dc, 1sc in corner ch sp, 1ch, 1sc in same ch sp, 4ch, miss next 5 dc, 1sc in next sc, 4ch, miss 5 dc, 1sc in next sc, *4ch, miss next 5 dc, 1sc in corner ch sp, 1ch, 1sc in same ch sp, 4ch, miss next 5 dc, 1sc in next sc, 4ch, miss 5 dc, 1sc in next sc; rep from * ending last rep ss in base of first 4-ch.

Round 6: Ss in first ch sp, 2ch (counts as first hdc), 4hdc in same ch sp, *[3hdc, 1ch, 3hdc] in next 1ch sp (corner), [5hdc in next ch sp] three times; rep from * ending last rep 5hdc in each of last 2-ch sps, join with a ss in top of first 2-ch.
Fasten off.

finishing

Block and press Squares lightly.
Lay out the squares with 4 squares across x 3 squares down, placing the colors randomly. With WS together make single crochet seams, joining the squares together into a panel for the front.
Repeat to make a panel for the back.
Make two panels of 3 x 1 squares for the sides.
Make one panel of 4 x 1 squares for the top.

With WS together, join one side of the top to the front and the other side to the back.
With WS together, add the first side panel, starting at the bottom edge of the front, along top edge and down back edge.
Repeat on other side.

Make up a lining in cotton fabric (see page 22, Method 1). Insert the lining into the Cozy with WS together. Turn over the hem of the lining at the bottom edge and pin in place around the edge of the crochet piece. Machine stitch or hand sew edge in place.

coloring pencil cozies

These look very cute in an office pen pot or as a gift for a child. The pencil cozy is a nice introduction to crocheting spirals in the round. These flowers are for the more experienced crocheter, but any flower will look just as good.

materials

Debbie Bliss Baby Cashmerino, 55% wool/33% acrylic/12% cashmere sport weight (lightweight DK) yarn
1 x 1¾oz (50g) ball—approx. 137yd (125m)—each of:

cozies
A: 02 Apple (green)
B: 68 Peach Melba (peach)
C: 01 Primrose (yellow)
D: 204 Baby Blue (blue)
E: 06 Candy Pink (pink)

flowers
E: 06 Candy Pink (pink)
F: 97 Speedwell (lilac)
G: 01 Primrose (yellow)
H: 68 Peach Melba (peach)

US size C/2 (2.5mm) crochet hook

gauge

Gauge is not important in this project.

finished measurement

Approx. length of a pencil: 6½in. (17cm)

abbreviations

approx. approximate(ly)
ch chain
dc double crochet
rep repeat
sc single crochet
ss slip stitch
st(s) stitch(es)
WS wrong side

special abbreviation

Picot—3ch, ss in first of 3-ch.

• •

cozy

(make 1 per pencil)
Using A, B, C, D , E, or F, make 2ch, 8sc in second ch from hook.
Work in a spiral making 1sc in each st until work measures 6½in. (17cm) or to length of pencil.
Fasten off.
Using a yarn sewing needle sew the first end closed.

flowers

(make 1 flower per cozy)
rose:
Using any Flower color yarn, make 36ch.
Round 1 (RS): 1dc in fourth ch from hook, [3ch, ss in first of 3-ch] (picot made), [1dc in same ch as previous dc made, 1 picot] twice, *1sc in next ch, 1 picot, [1dc in next ch, 1 picot] five times; rep from * once more, [1sc in next ch, 5dc in next ch] seven times, [1sc in next ch, 1dc, 1ch, 1dc in next ch] three times.
Fasten off leaving a long tail.
With WS facing, roll petals starting from the end of first petal and keeping the base level, pin in place and with a yarn sewing needle thread end and sew through base of petals several times to secure.

marigold:

Using any Flower color yarn, make 4ch, join with a ss to form a ring.

Round 1: 2ch (counts as first sc), 9sc in ring, ss in top of first 2ch. (10 sts)

Round 2: [5ch, ss in 2nd ch from hook and each of following 3-ch, ss in front strand only of next st] ten times. (10 petals)

Round 3: Bend petals forward and work into the remaining back loop of each st of first round. 2ch (counts as first sc), ss in first st, 1sc in each of next 9 sts, ss in top of first 2ch. (10 sts)

Round 4: [5ch, ss in 2nd ch from hook and each of following 3ch, ss in front strand only of st below, ss in front strand of the next st] ten times. (10 petals)

Round 5: Work as Round 3. (10 petals)

Round 6: Rep Round 4.
Fasten off.
Sew in ends.

finishing

Sew a Flower onto closed end of each pencil Cozy, and then slip Cozy onto a pencil.

cutlery cozies

Crochet for the table! Great for individual place settings and also a really good way to start learning how to bead.

materials

DMC Natura Just Cotton, 100% cotton fingering (4ply) yarn
1 x 1¾oz (50g) ball—approx. 169yd (155m) per ball—of:
N03 Sable (light gray)

US size E/4 (3.5mm) crochet hook

Approx. 114 Size 6 pale pink seed beads for each cozy

gauge

Approx 20 sts x 22 rows over a 4in. (10cm) square, working single crochet using US size E/4 (3.5mm) hook and Natura Just Cotton yarn.

finished measurement

Approx. 4in. (10cm) wide x 4½in. (11.5cm) long

note

The multiple is any number of sts (+ 1 for the base ch) (see page 18).

abbreviations

approx. approximate(ly)
ch chain
rep repeat
RS right side
sc single crochet
st(s) stitch(es)

special abbreviation

PB place bead—*On a WS row*, insert hook in next sc, yoh, pull yarn through (2 loops now on hook), slide bead up close to work, yoh, pull yarn through both loops on hook to complete beaded sc.

••

front

Thread approx. 114 beads onto yarn (see page 19).
Make 21ch.
Row 1 (RS): 1sc in second ch from hook, 1sc in each st to end. (20 sts)
Row 2: 1ch, 1sc in first st, *1sc/pb in next st, 1sc in next st; rep from * to last 2 sts, 1sc in each of last 2 sts. (20 sts)
Row 3: 1ch, 1sc in each st to end. (20 sts)
Row 4: 1ch, 1sc/pb in first st, 1sc in next st, *1sc/pb in next st, 1sc in next st; rep from * to end. (20 sts)
Row 5: Rep Row 3.
Rep rows 2–5 until 25 rows have been worked or work measures approx. 4½in. (11.5cm)
Fasten off.

back

Make 21ch.
Row 1 (RS): 1sc in second ch from hook, 1sc in each st to end. (20 sts)
Row 2: 1ch, 1sc in each st to end. (20 sts)
Rep Row 2 until 25 rows have been worked or work measures approx. 4½in. (11.5cm).
Fasten off.

finishing

Sew in ends. Place Front and Back with RS together. Sew side and bottom seams.
Turn RS out.

diary cozy

A great little cozy for keeping all your secrets safe. This fits a 2-page a day A5 diary, but would also fit an A5 one-page a day diary.

materials

cozy
Louisa Harding Cassia, 75% superwash wool/25% nylon light worsted (DK) weight yarn
1 x 1¾oz (50g) ball—approx. 144yd (132m)—each of:
A: 103 Chick (yellow)
B: 105 Glacier (blue)

hearts
Debbie Bliss Rialto DK, 100% merino wool light worsted (DK) weight yarn
1 x 1¾oz (50g) ball—approx. 115yd (105m)—of:
C: 12 Scarlet (red)

bookmark
DMC Natura Just Cotton, 100% cotton fingering (4ply) yarn
1 x 1¾oz (50g) ball—approx. 169yd (155m) per ball—of:
D: 03 Sable (light gray)

US size E/4 (3.5mm) crochet hook

Approx. 39 Size 6 pale pink seed beads

gauge
7 shell patts x 12 rows over 4in. (10cm) square, using US size E/4 (3.5mm) hook and Louisa Harding Cassia yarn.

finished measurement
9 x 6½ x 1in. (26 x 16.5 x 2.5cm)

abbreviations

approx. approximately
ch chain
ch sp chain space
dc double crochet
hdc half double crochet
patt(s) pattern(s)
rep repeat
RS right side
sc single crochet
ss slip stitch
st(s) stitch(es)
tr treble
WS wrong side

note

The multiple is 3 sts + 2 sts (+ 1 for the base ch) (see page 18).

back

(working from top to bottom)
Using A, make 36ch.

top edging:

Row 1: 1sc in second ch from hook, 1sc in each ch to end. (35 sts)
Cut yarn, do not fasten off.

Row 2 (WS): Join B, 2ch, miss first st *[1sc, 2ch, 1sc] in next st, miss next 2 sts; rep from * to end, 1hdc in 1-ch from Row 1.

Row 3 (RS): 3ch, *3dc in next 2-ch sp (shell made); rep from * to last st, 1dc in top of first 2-ch from previous row. (11 shells made)

Row 4: 2ch, *[1sc, 2ch, 1sc] in second dc of next shell; rep from * to last st, 1hdc in top of first 3-ch from previous row.

Rep Rows 3–4 until 25 rows are worked or work measures 9in. (23cm), ending on a Row 4.

Cut yarn, do not fasten off.

bottom edging:

Row 1: Join A, 1ch, 1sc in each of first 2 sts, *1sc in 2-ch sp, 1sc in each of next 2 sts; rep from * to end, ending, 1sc in top of 3-ch from previous row. (35 sts)

Row 2: 1ch, working in front loop of sts only, 1sc in each st to end. (35 sts)

Row 3: 1ch, working in back loop of sts only, 1sc in each st to end. (35 sts)

Row 4: 1ch, working in both loops of sts, 1sc in each st to end. (35 sts)

Row 5: Rep Row 4.

Row 6: 1ch, working in front loop of sts only, 1sc in each st to end. (35 sts)

Row 7: 1ch, working in back loop of sts only, 1sc in each st to end. (35 sts)

Row 8: 1ch, working in both loops of sts, 1sc in each st to end. (35 sts)

Fasten off.

front

(working from bottom to top)

Row 1 (WS): Join B in first 1ch of Row 8. 2ch, miss 2 sts, *[1sc, 2ch, 1sc] in next st, miss next 2 sts; rep from * to end, 1hdc in first 1-ch from previous row.

Row 2 (RS): 3ch, *3dc in next 2-ch sp (shell made); rep from * to last st, 1dc in top of first 2-ch from previous row.

Row 3: 2ch, *[1sc, 2ch, 1sc] in second dc of next shell; rep from * to last st, 1hdc in top of first 3-ch from previous row. (11 shells made)

Rep Rows 2–3 until 25 rows have been worked or work measures 9in. (23cm), ending on a Row 3.

Cut yarn, do not fasten off.

top edging:

Row 1 (RS): Join A, 1ch, 1sc in each of first 2 sts, *1sc in 2-ch sp, 1sc in each of next 2 sts; rep from * to last st, 1sc in last st, 1sc in top of 3-ch from previous row. (35 sts)

Row 2: Ss in each st to end.

Do not fasten off.

spine side 1:

With WS facing and working down first side.

Row 1: 1ch, 1sc in side of last row just made. Make approx 37sc evenly to first ridge of bottom edge, 2sc in edge of ridge, 2sc along base to next ridge, 2sc in edge of next ridge, make approx 37sc evenly from bottom of top of Back edging.

Row 2: 1ch, 1sc in back loop of each st to end.

Row 3: 1ch, 1sc in both loops of each st to end.

Do not fasten off.

Fold with WS together so single crochet seam is visible on RS.

Pin seam together starting by matching the bottom edges, 1ch, join using a single crochet seam.

Fasten off.

spine side 2:

With WS facing, join yarn in top of Back edge.

Repeat Spine Side 1.

finishing

Sew in ends.

Block and press on WS.

heart

(make 2)

Using C, make 4ch, join with a ss to form a ring.

Round 1: 3ch, [3tr, 3dc] into ring, [1ch, 1tr, 1ch] into ring, [3dc, 3tr] into ring, 3ch, join with a ss in ring.

Fasten off.

Sew one Heart in center of Front.

bookmark

Thread beads onto yarn D, make a chain approx. 13½in. (34cm) long, incorporating a bead on every alternate chain made. Sew second Heart onto one end.

suppliers

US STOCKISTS

Knitting Fever
(Debbie Bliss, Noro and Sirdar yarns)
Stores nationwide
www.knittingfever.com

The Knitting Garden
(Debbie Bliss, Noro and Sirdar yarns)
www.theknittinggarden.org

Webs
(yarn, crochet hooks, accessories, tuition)
75 Service Center Rd
Northampton, MA 01060
1-800-367-9327
www.yarn.com
customerservice@yarn.com

ACCESSORIES

A.C. Moore
(crochet hooks, accessories)
Online and east coast stores
1-888-226-6673
www.acmoore.com

Hobby Lobby
(crochet hooks, accessories)
Online and stores nationwide
1-800-888-0321
www.hobbylobby.com

Jo-Ann Fabric and Craft Store
(crochet hooks, accessories)
Stores nationwide
1-888-739-4120
www.joann.com

Michaels
(crochet hooks, beads)
Stores nationwide
1-800-642-4235
www.michaels.com

Unicorn Books and Crafts
(crochet hooks, accessories)
1-707-762-3362
www.unicornbooks.com
help@unicornbooks.com

UK STOCKISTS

Deramores
(yarn, crochet hooks, accessories)
 +44 1795 668144
www.deramores.com
customer.service@deramores.com

Designer Yarns
(distributor for Debbie Bliss yarns)
www.designeryarns.uk.com

Fyberspates Ltd
(yarn, crochet hooks)
+44 1829 732525
fyberspates@btinternet.com
www.fyberspates.co.uk

Hobbycraft
(yarn, crochet hooks)
Stores nationwide
+44 330 026 1400
www.hobbycraft.co.uk

Laughing Hens
(yarn, accessories)
The Croft Stables
Station Lane
Great Barrow
Cheshire CH3 7JN
+44 1829 740903
www.laughinghens.com
sales@laughinghens.com

John Lewis
(yarn, crochet hooks, accessories)
Stores nationwide
+44 1698 545454
www.johnlewis.com

TUITION

Nicki Trench
Crochet Club, workshops, accessories
www.nickitrench.com
nicki@nickitrench.com

ACCESSORIES

Addi Needles
(crochet hooks)
+44 1529 240510
www.addineedles.co.uk
addineedles@yahoo.co.uk

Debbie Abrahams Beads
(beads)
+44 115 855 1799
www.debbieabrahamsbeads.co.uk
beads@debbieabrahamsbeads.com

Knit Pro
(crochet hooks)
www.knitpro.eu

index

acknowledgments

It's impossible to produce a book like this without a fantastic group of people around me. Working on this project has been a great pleasure and I would like to say a big thank you to Anna Galkina from CICO Books who has been a joy to work with. Also a big thank you to Cindy Richards from CICO, who had the faith and confidence to commission me to work on this lovely book.

I am forever grateful and much appreciate all the help I have from my makers: Carolyn Meggison, Jenny Shore, and Sian Warr for their diligence, good humour and attention to detail, thanks also to Paula Watkins for her great embroidery skills; to Jean Burden for the gorgeous Dorset button on the Kindle Cozy, and to my mum for working through my patterns and crocheting some of the projects.

There are also thanks needed to the editors and checkers; Marie Clayton who edits most of my books and, as always, worked on this with great insight and efficiency, and also to Jane Czaja, the best pattern checker ever. Thanks also to Sally Powell at CICO, photographer Gavin Kingcome, stylists Sophie Martell and Nel Haynes, and to Barbara Zuniga for the book design.

I have used all my favorite yarns in this book and I'm very grateful to Rhiannon, Nicole, and Graeme at Designer Yarns for sending me the yarns so quickly and efficiently and also to Jeni at Fyberspates for letting me use her gorgeous Scrumptious yarn.

On a personal note, I would like to thank all my family for being so willing to get involved in the creative process and lending their honest opinions on the projects as they emerged. Thanks also to Victoria Solomon for her help before the project got started. And last but most certainly not least, a heart-felt thank you to JK for stepping in and kicking me into gear with an incredible amount of support and strength.